THE JOSHUA GENERATION

A Generation Rising to Claim Our Promised Land Destiny

Joseph Worth

Dedication

I dedicate this book to Jesus and the wonderful work He is doing on the earth. I also dedicate this book to my Mom, who dedicated me to the Lord on the delivery table and has faithfully prayed for me and poured into me throughout. I also dedicate this book to my wonderful wife Rebekah and to my Kingdom daughters Sydney and Sienna. The Lord has blessed me beyond measure.

Table of Contents

Acknowledgements

I want to thank the many mentors I have had along the way, but most importantly my family. I am so glad God has used you to teach me His ways more than any sermon or classroom ever could!

Introduction

On January 16, 1893, U.S. sailors were instructed to land on the island of Oahu in the Kingdom of Hawaii and take up positions at the U.S. Legation. 162 armed sailors and Marines aboard the USS *Boston* entered Honolulu Harbor and walked ashore with instructions to remain neutral. The sailors and Marines were instructed not to enter the palace grounds, take buildings, or even fire a shot. Their presence alone served to intimidate the royalist defenders to submit to their authority.

This *coup d'état* against Queen Liliuokalani led to the overthrow of the Kingdom of Hawaii. Foreigners living in Honolulu, primarily U.S. citizens who were subjects of the Kingdom of Hawaii, led the charge. It was American minister John L. Stevens who made the call for U.S. Marines to protect American interests in the islands. The Queen later concluded that "since the troops of the United States had been landed to support the revolutionists, by the order of the American minister, it would be impossible for us to make any resistance." The revolutionaries established the Republic of Hawaii and in 1898 Hawaii was fully annexed into the United States.

If you have ever been to Hawaii, I'm sure you've been struck with the island's excessive natural beauty. The massive mountain peaks, formed from volcanic eruptions in the middle of the ocean, provide a backdrop of extremes. The lush landscape, crystal clear waters and powerful crashing waves make it different from the other 49 U.S. states, but at the end of the day its people, laws and governance are all the same as the other states. In spite of the faint reminders of its historical culture, to me as a visitor it feels…American.

What if America was conquered by a larger, more powerful kingdom? Would we quickly understand how the concept of kingdom works? Would it be reflected in every corner of our land?

1

What has happened to the Kingdom of Hawaii is an example of what happens when a greater kingdom advances on a lesser one. In ancient conquests, upon victory, kings would erect images along each city's boundaries to show the citizens who was king and display what he looked like. This was to act as a reminder of who was in command. If this were to happen in our country today, our cities, counties, and states that currently operate under the laws and guidance of our country's system would come under new governance.

At every level, the laws of the new governance would apply. The former system would be transformed to resemble the larger, more powerful kingdom now in control. Ultimately, the entire system itself would be reformed to look like the new kingdom.

In these past conquests, however, transformation would only extend to the level of enforcement. The new laws and ordinances would have to be applied and enforced by conquerors and ambassadors of the conquering kingdom in order to have their full effect. So the transformation of the culture would be limited to the extent the ambassadors resembled the king and enforced his rule.

Let us consider the parallel. In the beginning, God created the heavens and the earth. The Genesis account states that He then made man in His image. He made us to be His image bearers, the ambassadors of His creation. His plan was to create us to resemble Him and to administer and enforce His ways on the earth. The natural outcome would be a planet that expressed His desires, the end of which would be complete transformation of the earth to mirror heaven.

The fall presents itself as the first hiccup in the experiment. Adam and Eve caving to temptation seemed to break mankind's ability to fulfill its role. However, an intervention was declared. The result of this intervention was for the image-bearers to be even more like their Creator. Destiny appeared delayed, but every biblical account pointed to a time when it would come into its fullness.

With an aggressive fast forward to our modern times, we know that some of the mystery of what occurred in the beginning has since been revealed. God's entrance in human form fulfilled many of the early promises, but the battle appears to still be raging. Promises yet to be fulfilled point to an even greater destiny still on the horizon.

Like the delegate who entered the shores of Hawaii signaled the end of an independent kingdom and advancement of a greater one, Jesus' triumph established the same. His victorious life, death, and resurrection announced to the earthly kingdom that a greater one has taken over. His win at Calvary ushered in the era of the preparation of His ambassadors. Almost 2,000 years have passed and the promises appear ready to come into their fullness. God's laws and ordinances of a never-ending Kingdom built on love and unity now await their full administration on the earth.

As we grow in Him, our experiences of this greater reality become tangible. Another realm is pregnant to break through. This heavenly realm is the destiny of a shared reality in our homes and gatherings, but we yet live in the tension between two realities. Our consistent experiences yet confirm the victory won so long ago.

Those who have tasted and seen that the Lord is good long for the manifestation of full restoration. As ambassadors in our homes, churches, communities and nations, we re-present the goodness of God to humanity. This nation of kings and priests spoken of by the prophets still appears as foolishness to the world, but change is upon us. Our advancement is coming into greater fullness and the revelation of His plans is unfolding before our very eyes. Heaven's ways are invading earth as never before, and what has been hidden until its appointed time is coming into full display for the watchful.

From the largest (Heaven and all it encompasses) to the smallest participants (our individual vessels) in God's Kingdom, our growing force of ambassadors are gaining alignment. We are allowing the ways of our King to transform our spirits, souls and bodies to His original intent. Our thinking and vision are being transformed to the realities of the greater governing Kingdom.

Our transformation means God's Kingdom is being advanced in our closest surroundings first—our families first, then our small gatherings together. Transformation that takes place in our homes, our churches, and communities will then bring our King's ways into our larger gatherings. As Christ unites us and His Holy Spirit orchestrates this work in concert across geographies, the individual Kingdom's functioning parts will influence the whole. Nations will rise to reflect the larger Kingdom of Heaven under God.

In this book we explore how our transformation is manifested as the Kingdom is formed inside of each of us. The work of His Spirit is to complete the work He started.

As we transform, we are enabled to help others until Christ is formed in them, starting a process that supernaturally multiplies. The end result is the unity of a growing body in the Spirit as leaven that works its way through the dough of the earth. This is the plan and story of our King, His Kingdom and the unity He has always intended for us. This is the story portrayed by Joshua that is coming into its fulfillment in our present era.

Prayer:

Holy Spirit, give me eyes to see and ears to hear. Please remove all preconceived thoughts and ideas that are not of you. Make way for me to see the story You are telling. You say the eyes are the windows to my soul and my soul has been corrupted by what I've seen and limited by what I've understood. God, you know ALL. Lead me into Your path and into my role on earth.

CHAPTER 1:
A Greater Calling

A restlessness pervades the battlefront. An awareness of where hope has faded, complacency replaced fervor, and hypocrisy pure love. There is a need, a desire, a longing for more. There are those who would rise to the call to overcome. There are those who no longer want to deny the destiny they are called to, the victory they are to claim, the ground they are to conquer. There is an unfulfilled longing in this generation, discontent with ways in which those in the church have fallen short and taken advantage, and a weariness of religious rituals. This is the least-churched generation, which yet exudes a profound interest in the spiritual. This draws them to seek out God without religious pretense. These people are exactly where God wants them to be. They are ready to experience what it is like to be empowered to live up to a greater calling than they thought possible.

Is this a longing in your heart? Will you rise to the challenge?

GOD'S INTENTION FROM THE BEGINNING

The one and only all-powerful Lord and Creator of all made us—people. He knit us together and gave us life. He did so for a purpose. We will start our journey by taking a glimpse at whether our lives currently reflect His purpose and intention, made possible by His sacrifice, or if we will find that we are living in much smaller stories. Our exploration will reveal if we live as ambassadors on a mission from an everlasting Kingdom or if we are building self-serving kingdoms that will crumble in time. It is a journey through time to discover we are designed to partner with God. With us stepping into our roles as conquerors with Him, the eternal King of an everlasting Kingdom will accomplish His perfect plan.

Does something inside you quiver at the thought of being a conqueror? Is this fear driven by the misuse of power you experienced in the past? Do your own feelings of insecurity and self-doubt or doctrines long held onto keep you from your destiny? Allow the Lord to help you suspend such preconceptions as we explore His undeniably good plans to redeem the earth.

Embedded in an all-too-familiar passage, the Bible opens with a reference to God's intention for a people He created to one day rule:

"In the beginning, God created the heavens and the earth...Then God said, 'Let us make mankind in our image, in our likeness, <u>so that they may rule </u>over the fish in the sea and the birds in the sky, over the livestock and all the wild animals, and over all the creatures that move along the ground.' So God created mankind in his own image, in the image of God he created them; male and female he created them. God blessed them and said to them: 'Be fruitful and increase in number; <u>fill the earth and subdue it</u>. <u>Rule over</u> the fish in the sea and the birds in the sky and over every living creature that moves on the ground.'" (Genesis 1:1, 1:26-28)

In God's very first recorded words on mankind's role, we find these profound words: "so that they may rule." His intention is made clear in His counsel, among His own fellowship. His intention in making mankind was so that we may rule. A few verses later, He addresses us for the very first time. He provides His initial command to "Fill the earth... subdue it... rule over [it]..." The Hebrew is *radah*. Some translations use the word "dominion." It is a royal word associated with kingship.

God's intention, made clear right from the very beginning, was exactly what He said. Here is a paraphrase: "Let's make mankind to be like Me so they will rule on this new earth I've created, in the same way that I rule everything I've ever made." Let us agree He made us like Him so we could do what He does, so the earth would be a good place.

PURPOSE THROUGH PERVERSION

We know what happens next. It shattered the beautiful fellowship Adam and Eve got from their Father, "walking together in the cool of the day." One can only imagine the beauty of the world before the fall. Words cannot express the splendor of this backdrop. A Father with a son and daughter and endless territory to discover...together.

I envision an unrushed environment of questions, answers, mystery, and wonder. The questions were meant to be answered by the Father, but the environment of discovery left room for wondering, that led to doubt. Why was this other tree in the garden? Why would our Father allow this type of risk? Why even create a bad tree with such a temptation?

Our heart's deep longing for Eden often does not allow us such wonderings. Our systems and theology leave little room for doubt, which can only display much feared weakness. When combined with fear, the enemy can roll doubts and questions into unbelief, so we shut it down.

We divorce ourselves from our own journey of discovery in the name of safety and self-preservation. But with our challenge, which is lodged deep inside the heart of all overcomers, comes a day of reckoning. A time when the call to separate from the pack and take risks beckons us to a land of discovery. Steps of faith ensue, and suddenly we find ourselves burning the very ship that brought us to shore. Like Adam, our questions beg for answers as well. Why would God take such a dramatic risk with His creation? Why was a choice for evil allowed? Perhaps these questions are exactly what He wants from us on our journey? Perhaps even the answers were designed for discovery? He made us to be like Him, "so come let us reason with Him" to learn His ways.

We learn from the scriptures that Father God is training kings. Temptation is necessary. Options are necessary. The backdrop of genuine character and powerful decision making is choice. Just as princes are not given thrones upon birth, a new creation (even made in the image of a great and perfect King) must grow into its role. In a perfectly designed scenario, a prince would be trained under the loving care and guidance of a good king. As the prince's father, the king would teach royalty and train his son to conduct himself in a kingly manner. The prince would learn the ways of his father's kingdom, be trained in fighting, study strategies, understand the administration of his father's resources, and prepare to govern well the increasing responsibilities that were given to him. Then, at the appointed time, the son would assume his role on the throne.

We also learn Father God is training His overcomers to be priests. The first training lesson on this role occurs after the fall, when we see the King Himself first demonstrate the role of a priest. In Genesis 3:21, He makes a sacrifice to provide a covering to clothe Adam and Eve in their nakedness. The first blood sacrifice was made and the first blood covering was provided. The covering was provision not only to cover their nakedness, but their sin. Their fig leaves, as the work of their own hands, were not sufficient. As a good Father, God took it on Himself to provide the covering. His heart for provision and restoration was on full display. We later see the blood sacrifice and covering as a type and shadow of later priestly fulfillments.

The revelation of God's plans for His kings and priests comes with the very next verse, after providing a covering for original sin. God said, "The man has now become like one of us, knowing good and evil."

Wow! Could this statement be connected to His initial intent? "Let us make mankind in our image, in our likeness." How is it that we got there through disobedience? Did we truly become more like Him through original sin? This seems preposterous, based on my Sunday school upbringing. Let us look at our enemy's role before we can settle the matter.

Jesus said Satan was a liar from the beginning. He called him the father of lies. Lies are most powerful and effective when mixed with truth.

We will examine the pattern in Satan's first recorded words to mankind, the lying from the beginning Jesus referenced:

"Did God really say, 'You must not eat from any tree in the garden'?" (Genesis 3:1)

Satan's first words were indeed crafty, creating doubt by questioning God's good intention. He states the truth, but perverts it.

"For God knows that when you eat from it your eyes will be opened, and you will be like God, knowing good and evil." (Genesis 3:5)

Now Jesus said Satan was a liar from the beginning, but He did not say Satan does not use truth. Based on God's response, "The man has now become like one of us, knowing good and evil," we see that Satan was using truth to convince Eve to eat the fruit.

There is yet more to this story. The implications of the re-interpretation of this long-told story through the lens of God's intention for us to be like Him are staggering. We see the opponent being artfully used by the Master to accomplish His intended purpose. As a proverbial tool in the Master's hands, the adversary plays his necessary role.

Could there be more to God's intentions for temptation as well? For the fall of mankind and even the tempter himself? God made us to be like Him, then immediately after the fall He confesses we have indeed become more like Him. Oh, the mystery of God's wisdom!

Let me be so bold as to say we had encountered evil, and evil served its first purpose by causing us to need a covering. Evil was also revealing its overall design here in our first encounter. God was using it to teach, train and provide for a people that were created to be like Him.

Going a step further, God was showing that our struggle with—and eventual victory over—an opponent was going to be the key to becoming like Him. How do we know this? Right here in this same story, God names the outcome.

"I will put enmity between you and the woman, and between your offspring and hers; <u>he will crush your head</u>, and you will strike his heel." (Genesis 3:15)

God foretells Satan's hatred of and future war against women, calling it enmity (being actively opposed to). He then makes it clear one day Satan's head will be crushed by a male of her offspring.

We may have lost our ability to take dominion over evil and the earth after this fall, but provision was built right into it. Even though mankind was deceived into setting up kingdoms in our own image, one day this would come to an end. We could no longer be like God after the fall, but God used it to pull back a veil on His plan. Another veil remained, and it wasn't to lift until it was torn. God's plan of redemption through Jesus, to crush the enemy's head, was to become like us. Why did this have to be? To make a way for us to be more like Him.

In order to carry His image and be true ambassadors of His Kingdom, we would need to see and experience what it looked like for Him to reign over an enemy. We would also need His provision for doing so. In Christ, we received our instruction, our apprenticeship training, and our provision (His Spirit). This "activation" would enable us to be like He was on the earth.

JESUS AS THE ULTIMATE CONQUEROR

Jesus died to free us to live as He always intended. His form of conquering demonstrated something radically different from what man could ever conceive. He called us to death and in return offered us abundant life. This life enabled us to finally execute on His eternal plan. To redeem the earth and bring it under His rule.

God's Kingdom had come, but He also taught us to pray for its full entrance. Death was conquered to put an end to our enemy's foothold, but salvation from death was not the end of the matter. In demonstrating a victorious life, He unlocked our destiny and beckoned us to lean into it.

He laid out a path for us to live as God has always intended. This path is more than simply natural, it is supernatural in our earthly context, and the standard operating procedure in heaven's. He showed us the way. It is not the way of safety or self-preservation, but the only way to the life He intended for us.

A GREATER WAY

So what are we, the church, doing with this opportunity? Have we mixed in our own ways or truly leaned into all He unlocked for us? The answer is too much of the former and not enough of the latter. A tree is known by its fruit, so our addition of mixture (leaven) is always on full display in harvest season.

Many have used Jesus to lift themselves up. In doing so they've built kingdoms, gained influence and enjoyed their fleeting rewards. The accumulation of abuses in His name, however, have had an effect on the masses. Many believe God now needs to be re-presented to the world outside of a church context where many of the abuses have occurred. Are we open to it?

Roadblocks of pride, heritage, and fear of change exist in the mainstream denominations. Will God raise up among the foolish another movement that will provoke the broader church to jealousy and change? If all is fair in love and war, we can be assured God will do what it takes to get His bride ready. The body of Christ can shift its focus from constructing buildings to building God's Kingdom, since they have been called, but a seismic shift will be needed.

The bold conquerors will need to arise in the power of the Spirit. As the light of the world and salt of the earth, a generation of unshakable servant champions will walk in the love, power, and authority of Jesus to bring about this coming shift.

We were not left alone to carry out this great calling. God's plan was always to raise up His temple in man. The manifestations of this fullness will not at first be for the masses, but for the remnant.

There is a generation who will come to the place of ruling and reigning before the others. They are called to lead the charge that brings the change. Their lives will bring us all into the destiny God has always intended for His creation. The destiny of coming out of the wilderness, completing the conquest of evil and bringing the fullness of heaven to earth.

CHAPTER 2:
A Wilderness Journey

On November 18, 2012 Jose Salvador Alvarenga set sail on an overnight fishing trip off the coast of Mexico with fishing partner Ezequiel Córdoba. Shortly after their departure they were ravaged by a storm for five consecutive days. During the storm their boat took on damage and a broken motor and lost equipment left them in a lost and helpless position in the Pacific Ocean.

The two men did their best to shield themselves from the sun, wind and rain with in an overturned ice box. They crouched together under the small shade, but the time and elements took their toll. Within two months Alvarenga could only watch as Córdoba succumbed to the harsh elements. After speaking to the corpse to keep himself company, eventually Alvarenga would lower his deceased friend into the ocean.

Surviving on a diet of raw sea turtles and birds and the occasional fish, Alvarenga started to go crazy. But that's when a deep desire to survive kicked in. He figured out how to fish with his hands, one knife and a machete. He drank turtle blood when it didn't rain. He ate birds he kept prisoners and even played soccer against the birds with the carcass of a blowfish, using the center-line of the boat as the goal.

After 438 days at sea and floating an estimated 9,000 miles, Alvarenga washed up 2,375 miles off the coast of Hawaii in the tiny Marshall Islands. Confused and disheveled somehow he survived the bizarre and certainly unplanned journey to his unknown but beautiful island destination.

As I pondered the almost 2,000-year journey for the church since Pentecost, I was reminded of the aimless floating of Alvarenga. Not to be too harsh, but the similarities between the church's journey and the Israelites' 40-year journey in the wilderness are even striking. Both journeys began with signs and wonders, a promise, and radical deliverance. They each started off so well. The children of Israel sang one of the greatest worship songs in history after crossing through the Red Sea and Peter, fresh off his denial of Jesus, delivered one of the best sermons ever preached at Pentecost.

Going a step further, these parallel journeys even seemed a lot like my own as a Christian. Dedicated to the Lord on the delivery table, great grandson of a famous rabbi turned evangelist, born on the day of atonement, son of a deacon, "saved" at age seven, I started off so well! But the lack of genuine signs of life in the church, the dullness of obedience and attraction to the world led me into a double life of aimless wandering. Then, somehow on November 18th 2012, the very day Alvaranga set sail in Mexico, the seed of true sonship was awakened in me.

As I rejoiced in learning the love of God for what felt like the first time, I also marveled at the 30 years I spent wandering. How could I have learned so much yet missed it entirely? I suppose this question brings us back to the comparison between the children of Israel in the wilderness and the church of the last 2,000 years.

What happened? Their journeys began with such promise! They saw the miracles of God, heard His voice and experienced His very presence. But just as quickly as both were launched, division came. They grumbled. Israel complained to Moses (who as the nation's deliverer of the time foreshadowed Jesus) and the early church debated doctrines. They griped about God and worried about what their eyes saw and minds perceived.

Two journeys. Two culminations. One complete, one completing. In reviewing the similarities, I can't help but believe one speaks to the other. Just as Israel wondered why they wandered so long, it's challenging to understand why God would pour out his Spirit and then allow the church to languish so long. Where did the power go? Was it intended for small corners and pockets or was it designed for all to see? Where is the victory? Where are the Joshuas and the Calebs?

Just like the Israelites in the wilderness, the body of believers we call the church has been given a promise. The promise is not only completion of the journey, but victory. We have been promised an eternity of ruling as kings and priests with Him. All the promises are now in print for our eyes to see. This is not only for the trained and educated, but for anyone who would lay claim to their true identity.

As I wrestled with the uncomfortable truth that His church has seemingly floundered, rather than building on its early purity and promise, the Lord met me in my discomfort. He connected the dots for me to see how our almost 2,000-year church journey was His plan all along.

ISRAEL'S JOURNEY

On their geographically short journey from Egypt to the Promised Land, the Israelites experienced God. He parted the sea, they were covered by His cloud, and they enjoyed His manna, to name some of His provision. The nature of the miracles proved the Lord was not only their deliverer, but their provider.

Yet, with it all, they did not want a direct relationship with Him. Why? The simple answer is fear. Let's see how fear dictated their opportunity to commune with the Lord.

"When you heard the voice out of the darkness, while the mountain was ablaze with fire, all the leaders of your tribes and your elders came to me. And you said, 'The LORD our God has shown us his glory and his majesty, and we have heard his voice from the fire. Today we have seen that a person can live even if God speaks with them. But now, why should we die? This great fire will consume us, and we will die if we hear the voice of the LORD our God any longer. For what

mortal has ever heard the voice of the living God speaking out of fire, as we have, and survived? Go near and listen to all that the LORD our God says. Then tell us whatever the LORD our God tells you. We will listen and obey.'" (Deuteronomy 5: 23-27)

It is here the people select Moses to listen to the Lord on their behalf. Rather than hearing the Lord directly for themselves to have a relationship with Him, they begged for a man with credentials for the job to stand between them and God. Like Adam and Eve, they were afraid, so they hid. This time behind a man.

Also like Adam and Eve, the children of Israel recognized the power of God. Instead of allowing it to be a healthy fear to train them, their fear caused separation. It could have led them to repentance and a direct relationship, but it drove a wedge. Their desire was not to know God Himself, but simply to enjoy the benefits and protection of being His people. So when their outcomes didn't line up with what they expected, they revolted. God's response, separated from a personal relationship with them, was usually to reintroduce fear to restore order (He used snakes, plagues, other nations, etc to train them in this manner).

Genuine transformation through a relationship was available, but without it, the children of Israel remained unchanged. Upon appointing Moses, motivated by fear, they promised to "listen and obey" to appease God. Without the trust and faith that come from a relationship with Him, they lacked the ability to actually follow through.

Denying the opportunity to know and love God intimately cost Israel dearly. The repeat of this mistake has equally damaged the church. God designed us so that our lives will not work apart from a genuine relationship with Him. Jesus said "If you love Me you will keep My commandments." It is hard to love one you haven't gotten to know. The inverse of Jesus' statement is also true. "If you don't know me, you can't love me and follow my ways." So this is where Israel, and in many ways the church, has come up short. Without a love relationship with God, we cannot keep His commands. Israel's commitment to God would come crashing down before they had even laid eyes on the commands He wrote for them.

WORSHIPING HIM, NOT OUR UNDERSTANDING OF HIM

"When the people saw that Moses was so long in coming down from the mountain, they gathered around Aaron and said, 'Come, make us gods who will go before us. As for this fellow Moses who brought us up out of Egypt, we don't know what has happened to him.'

"Aaron answered them, 'Take off the gold earrings that your wives, your sons and your daughters are wearing, and bring them to me.' So all the people took off their earrings and brought them to Aaron. He took what they handed him and made it into an idol cast in the shape of a calf, fashioning it with a tool. Then they said, 'This is your god, Israel, who brought you up out of Egypt.'

"When Aaron saw this, he built an altar in front of the calf and announced, 'Tomorrow there will be a festival to the LORD.' So the next day the people rose early and sacrificed burnt offerings and presented fellowship offerings." (Exodus 32:1-6)

Notice the motivation. Moses was taking too long. They feared that something had happened to him, leaving them stranded. They did not trust that God was in control of the situation. The people sought a god they could see and control, so they devised a way to make a god out of their own offerings. Since they suffered a loss to make the idol from the treasures they brought from Egypt, it seemed like a good idea. The golden calf was a god of their own understanding. They made it in the Lord's name and sang and danced about the Lord's exploits as they worshipped it, giving it credit for the Lord's victories of leading them from Egypt.

In many ways, Aaron and the golden calf experiment is representative of the wilderness journey the church has been on.

We have elevated men to stand in the place of Aaron and Moses. Instead of having a direct relationship, we have chosen pastors, church attendance and religious duty to fill the void. In order for us to come out of the wilderness and take the territory God has promised us, we need to hear His voice and know Him. Our attentiveness to His voice and our love relationship with Him produce the faith required to enter in and remain.

"For whatever is born of God overcomes the world. And this is the victory that has overcome the world—our faith." (1 John 5:4)

Faith is the product of relationship. And faith is the very victory that has overcome (conquered) the world! We can meet with God and He will speak faith into us. As we grow in our relationship and the faith that results from it, we overcome. This isn't speculation, it is fact. John wrote this passage over 1,900 years ago as though it had already happened. His writing speaks to a future time of fulfillment.

What, then, stands in the way of us? It is often easier for us to worship the God of our own understanding than worshipping God Himself. Our systems are comfortable, predictable and easily touchable, while God can feel remote, risky and invisible. The only way we will step into His victory is if we choose to know Him and embrace the risk and mystery. It takes faith to lean into the unknown and open up to discovery, but as we do, He will confirm every step towards our destiny. In Israel's case, we learn that only two had the faith to inherit the Promised Land.

ADVANCING TOWARDS THE PROMISE

As Israel progressed beyond Sinai, on through the wilderness under Moses, they came to the border of the Promised Land. Like the aggressive advances of the early church, they had an opportunity to seize destiny.

Joshua and Caleb saw a good land, a land flowing with milk, honey, and food of an unusual sort: giant humans. He labeled these giants as sustenance. "They are food for us," Joshua claimed. He stood on the promise of the Lord that the land was theirs, so he believed the obstacles in their way must have only been there to strengthen them. So convinced were Joshua and Caleb that following God was the only way, this was their response when Israel expressed a lack of faith due the size of their opponents:

"Joshua son of Nun and Caleb son of Jephunneh, who were among those who had explored the land, tore their clothes and said to the entire Israelite assembly, 'The land we passed through and explored is exceedingly good. If the Lord is pleased with us, he will lead us into that land, a land flowing with milk and honey, and will give it to us. <u>Only do not rebel against the Lord. And do not be afraid of the people of the land, because we will devour them. Their protection is gone, but the Lord is with us. Do not be afraid of them.</u>'" (Numbers 14:6-9)

The Israelites in the wilderness did not heed the words of Joshua and Caleb. While Joshua trusted in the Lord with all his heart, the Israelites leaned on their own understanding. The children of Israel experienced the truth of Hebrews 11:6 that without faith it is impossible to please God, and thus, the millions of Israelites that were delivered from the hands of Pharaoh perished in the wilderness.

On the other hand, as a result of their faith, Joshua and Caleb became the only two of the original crew that would one day enjoy the promise. Their trust of the Lord exceeded their own understanding. The rest of the Israelites could have marched straight into the land of promise, but they did not have the faith to enter in. Fear, a product of not knowing the Lord, held them back.

Had the Lord given up on His people? Far be it from God to do so. Although Moses and those of Israel who refused to follow God's best for their lives perished, Joshua was appointed to lead the warriors of the next generation of Israelites into the Promised Land.

Are we willing to think of this in the context of the church of the last 2,000 years? We have not only the historical account of the resurrection, but the promise of our own! Without the faith produced by knowing Him, however, we will not fulfill the real great commission to redeem the earth. Without faith, we will not put all enemies under the Lord's feet.

If we trust Him and hear His voice, however, we will be led by Him into our inheritance. Our destiny will be unlocked. In order to avoid becoming like the Israelites who did not inherit the promise, we must choose Him. We must consider the mistakes of those who have gone before us and go all-in on knowing Jesus.

Let us learn this lesson so we can boldly exit the wilderness. Let us cast off the old structures and systems and choose His presence. Let us be like Joshua and Caleb who chose to trust Him over their own understanding and stand in His promises before they saw how they would be fulfilled.

We have the full Word available to us. We see the stories of the early saints. We have countless records of God's promises and provision. We know the Lord's requirement that we should have the faith to enter and possess the land. Let us now allow Him to develop in us what is required to enter in.

Up until now, many of our personal lives have been lived in retreat rather than advance. This was not the story of the miraculous early church, our earthly example of what the Lord is doing again in our generation.

A REQUIRED TIME OF TRAINING

The Israelites could have marched straight into the Promised Land if they only had believed God, yet it was appointed unto a time and for a future generation. The early church could have continued its parabolic growth and put every enemy under His feet, but it was appointed unto a time and future generation.

"These were all commended for their faith, yet they did not receive what was promised. God had planned something better for us, so that together with us they would be made perfect." (Hebrews 11:39-40)

I love how this very culmination of the great faith hall of fame chapter in Hebrews ends in verse 40. It is both symbolic and representative. It speaks to the faith of our ancestors who died waiting for the fulfillment of the promise. At the end of 40 years, the next generation of Israelites in the wilderness did enter in.

As we learn God's heart for forgiveness, we even see it in His calendar. Even His calendar has forgiveness built right into it. Per God's instructions, every 50th year, the children of Israel were to celebrate a Jubilee. At this time all slaves were to be released, all debts cancelled and "everyone was to return to their own property" (Leviticus 25:13). Since the Jubilee is a "Sabbath of Sabbaths," for the people, it is representative of 7 Sabbaths (7 x 7), but was to be celebrated in the 50th year after the 7 Sabbaths were completed.

The 50th year also represents the 1st year of the next cycle, so 40 Jubilees equates to 1,960 years (40 x 49). If Jesus died in 33 AD, then 40 Jubilees brings us to 1993. So the period of 40 Jubilees since Pentecost compares well with the 40 years in the desert.

The parting words from Moses apply well to our 40 Jubilees since Pentecost.

"Remember how the Lord your God led you all the way in the wilderness these forty years, to humble and test you in order to know what was in your heart, whether or not you would keep his commands. He humbled you, causing you to hunger and then feeding you with manna, which neither you nor your ancestors had known, to teach you that man does not live on bread alone but on every word that comes from the mouth of the Lord. Your clothes did not wear out and your feet did not swell during these forty years. Know then in your heart that as a man disciplines his son, so the Lord your God disciplines you." (Deuteronomy 8:2-5)

As the church, we have been humbled, we have been tested, and our hearts have too often been exposed for the wrong motives. We too often have settled for the manna of our own hands rather than the true bread that comes from His mouth. But the Lord has used this as our time of discipline and preparation for His fullness. It is hopeful to know that after the 40 years, a generation finally entered in, because it speaks to our destiny. Although our wilderness journey has often felt like victory was in question rather than secured, we can stand on the promise.

Notice the church did not enter directly into the Promised Land after Passover and Pentecost—instead, the wilderness. The children of Israel did not enter in after their original Passover miracle in Egypt—instead, the wilderness. They had a chance to enter directly in, but they chose not to believe Joshua and Caleb's good report. After their rebuke, they tried to enter in by their own strength, but failed. God warned Moses that it was not His will for them to enter, so rather than entering, 39 more years of preparation ensued.

"Tell them, 'Do not go up and fight, because I will not be with you. You will be defeated by your enemies.'" (Deuteronomy 1:42)

The children of Israel had repented and were ready to go! But God did not relent. We could say God was punishing them for their unbelief, or we could recognize God's sovereignty and agree it was not His plan for them to enter in. The church also tried to enter in by their own strength, but the 40-Jubilee time of training and preparation was still required. This is all to establish there are more than a few significant parallels between Israel's 40 years in the desert and the church era since Pentecost.

Fast forwarding through the Israelites' journey in the desert, we learn the next generation finally entered in. We also learn they did not see the fullness of God's plan after entering in and conquering many nations. They represented a type and shadow of a future generation that would enter and remain.

God's instruction to the children of Israel was for them to destroy every living soul, every carved image, and even the livestock in most cases. Israel's job was to cleanse the land completely. Jesus gave instructions to love, forgive, and teach all the nations to obey His ways. Two instructions from the same God at polar opposite ends of the spectrum. The lion and the lamb, the first and the last, the King and the suffering servant, the God of both mercy and judgment again paradoxically displays His plan with extreme contrast. Thus, Israel's demonstration of entering in under Joshua was to enlighten a future generation to enter in under the power and Sonship of Yeshua.

The current Joshua Generation of faith is the one the initial Joshua pointed to. After 40 Jubilees, we are now peering over the banks of the Jordan into the Promised Land with faith and anticipation. While gazing on our opponents and the obstacles, we remember God's promises and are strengthened. We now see them in a clearer light, and Yeshua's instructions, demonstrations and power provide our fuel and guidance. The enemy opposition is merely food for the journey.

As we enter the Jordan to cross, just as the Lord stopped the waters for our ancestors, He will make the way as our faith causes us to proceed. Once crossing over to possess the land, the waters again returned for Israel. There was no way for them to return to the wilderness. We are strengthened to know that when we cross over, we are never going back.

"No one who puts a hand to the plow and looks back is fit for service in the kingdom of God." (Luke 9:62)

The Kingdom is about constant advance. We are advancing and entering into the fullness of the Kingdom God has always intended for us.

THE WILDERNESS CHURCH

"Today, if you hear his voice, do not harden your hearts. For if Joshua had given them rest, God would not have spoken later about another day. There remains, then, a Sabbath-rest for the people of God; for anyone who enters God's rest also rests from their works, just as God did from his. Let us, therefore, make every effort to enter that rest, so that no one will perish by following their example of disobedience." (Hebrews 4:7-11)

The provision of the Spirit was to usher in an era of rest, but as has been established, we are still yet to see its fulfillment. Instead, we have seen divisions among our churches and partial moves of Spirit and Truth with few examples of the power that comes when Spirit and Truth are together. As John 4:24 reveals, "God is spirit, and his worshipers must worship in the Spirit and in truth." Rather than an endorsement from the Lord of our structures, we see an admonishment.

In Revelation 18:4, the Lord implores us to "come out of her, my people." We are His people and we are in something He wants us to come out of. The context of the Revelation passage is Babylon. Babylon has a long history. It is the place where men built a tower to reach the heavens and the place where religion sprang from, during Israel's captivity. In Revelation, we learn its resurgence besets the children of God.

With that backdrop, let us review what happened only shortly after the original outpouring and establishment of the church. It is important to know what we are coming out of, so the following is a brief review of institutional church history.

The church grew amidst a backdrop of mixture, opposition, and the martyrdom of the faithful as higher criticism and reasoning came into the faith. By 250 A.D., widespread violent universal persecution of Christianity by the Romans had intensified. The reason for the persecution was mainly because the Roman Empire had begun to crumble and the emperor was calling for absolute submission to his authority. Christians could not offer this submission, because Jesus was their King.

By 312 A.D., Christianity seemed to have caught its biggest break. After seeing a vision of the cross and hearing the words "go forth and conquer," the Emperor Constantine embraced Christianity. Yes, in the very context of "conquering," Constantine eventually named Christianity the official religion of the land.

Unfortunately, the Roman form of conquering did not follow God's Psalm 72, Isaiah 61, and Matthew 28's principles of caring for the broken hearted. And although Christianity's adoption as a religion initially ended much of the persecution of the era, its very nature changed in every way.

As the purity of their unity gave way to an institutional church, the religious hierarchy grew in stature. Persecutions of true disciples of Jesus grew as well. What is considered the "Dark Ages" ensued, with an estimated 1,000 years of pain and torment for those who were loyal to the true King's domain (Kingdom = king's domain).

It was a time in history comparative to the time of King Saul, whose pride and insecurities fueled a relentless hunt to kill David. Saul presided over a regime that used the nation's resources senselessly to track down a true lover of God. The Roman rule of this age did the same. They pursued and crushed the David's with such fervor that almost all true worshippers not in hiding were snuffed out.

Empowered by partnership with the governments of the nations, those in power did their best to keep the people in fear and ignorance. Printed Bibles in any form were scarce and rarely found in a language other than Latin. The struggle became so great one historian records:

"This was a time, when not only was the Bible banned, but literacy in general was prohibited and frowned upon. Very few

people during this time knew how to read or write. The Institutional Church was determined that the less knowledge that people had, the easier it would be to rule them. 'Only ten percent of people in the Roman Empire could read...and those were generally in the wealthy upper classes.'" (Source: *River of God*, Gregory J. Riley, 2001, pp. 66)

The Institutional Church (the only real church of its day) itself even admitted this in her own law on several occasions during this period. One such example is found in The Council of Tarragona of 1234 in its second canon, ruling:

"No one may possess the books of the Old and New Testaments, and if anyone possesses them he must turn them over to the local bishop within eight days, so that they may be burned..." – *The Church Council of Tarragona, 1234 A.D., in the 2nd Canon.* (Source: *Historie de la Bible en France*, D. Lortsch, 1910, p.14)

The consequences of misalignment with the doctrines of the institutional church were grave. Another historian records:

"It is estimated by careful and credible historians, that more than fifty millions of the human family, have been slaughtered for the crime of heresy by persecutors within the church, an average of more than forty thousand religious murders for every year..." (Source: *History of Romanism*, John Dowling, pp. 541, 542. New York: 1871).

Conscious observers who knew Christian history at this point must have been wondering where the Holy Spirit was. Was He akin to Jose Alvarenga, floating aimlessly from His departure point? Were things too lost and too far gone for hope to remain? When the days seemed the darkest, the light shined through. In 1517 a shift occurred. The publishing of Martin Luther's Ninety-Five Theses and the emergence of the Protestant reformation welcomed back Truth. The term "protestant" was derived from those who openly "protested" the practices of the institutional church.

Recognizing his-tory as "His Story," God saw fit to have the printing press and widespread translation of the Word into the languages of the people coincide with this reformation. This brought about the first seismic shift in the *ecclesia* since the original outpouring and a creative renaissance right along with it.

The enlightenment church, modern church, and post-modern church all followed along with outpourings of the Spirit, revivals and pseudo-reformations. The earth has since come alive with creativity that can only be attributed to the Spirit's outpouring. The Kingdom has since been accelerating at a pace not seen since the early church.

It is now believed that more people have come to Christ since the Azusa Street outpouring in Los Angeles in 1906 than in the 1,900 years before! "All of creation is indeed anxiously awaiting the sons of God to be revealed." (Romans 8:19). Each generation draws us closer to this fulfillment.

Even yet, the statistics demonstrate we are missing the fullness of our inheritance:

- Roughly same number of marriages in church and secular culture end in divorce.

- Research shows the rates for drug, alcohol and pornography addictions are the same inside and outside the church.

- Only 15% of the 360,000 churches in the U.S. are growing.

- Only 2-5% of the growing churches are growing by new conversions to Christ.

- 90% of evangelical church members do not share their faith.

- 50% of all evangelical churches did not have a single convert last year.

- Only 51% of pastors and 19% of confessed born-again believers have what is defined as a biblical world view (absolute moral truths exist; the Bible is totally accurate in all principles it teaches; Satan is considered to be a real being or force and not merely symbolic; a person cannot earn their way into heaven; Jesus lived a sin free life on earth; and God is the all-knowing, all-powerful creator of the world who still rules the universe today).

- 70% of people raised in the church leave it between the ages of 18-23.

- Christians on average tithe 2-3% of their income to their church or another form of Kingdom work.

(Source: Barna Research Group, 2008-2016)

"What is mankind that you are mindful of them, a son of man that you care for him? You made them a little lower than the angels; you crowned them with glory and honor and put everything under their feet." In putting everything under them, God left nothing that is not subject to them. Yet at present we do not see everything subject to them." (Hebrews 2:5-8)

We do not yet see our fulfillment of our higher calling in Christ to the earth. There is yet a time to come when we will cross over into the Promised Land and put everything under His feet. We are now in the wilderness in preparation for this time. I believe it is fast approaching. I believe the Lord is now revealing mysteries from His Law and Word that our forefathers have long awaited to see and understand.

The culture of heaven is still currently breaking through to the earth. Our King has given us the edict to be salt and light to this world. He has set aside our provision, awaiting a generation that has the faith to pull it down.

At our current hour, the mixture Paul warned about is still mixing in. Was God's intention a languishing, defeated family or a victorious one? Too many structures still elevate man, and too many of us are still deceived by the masquerading angel of light.

We have too often conformed to the pattern of this world rather than allowing the Lord to transform us. Knowing truth and walking by His Spirit are the only answer.

Our King's famous Sermon on the Mount tells us that in the Kingdom, change first starts within each of us. Before change comes to the church, the Kingdom must first be formed within each of us and within our homes.

The very foundation of the Kingdom has to be our continual, unbroken fellowship with the King. As we proceed, we will explore this very foundation and how it is to be built upon.

GOD'S PEOPLES' PLACE IN HIS PLAN

The Lord is waiting. He is waiting for His kings and priests to rule and reign over His enemy with Him. He is waiting to return with the fullness of His Kingdom. He desires a people completing their assignment on earth—a people with the faith and trust of Joshua and Caleb who led His people out of the wilderness.

Our land of opposition, like the giants inhabiting the land promised to Israel, is designed to strengthen us. Our destiny has been promised, but the promise is yet to be fulfilled. His inheritance is our destiny. The inheritance is part of His unconditional promise and eternal plan to "put all enemies under His feet."

Our Lord, however, does not wait idly. He who appointed His people to accomplish His purpose is actively guiding and empowering them to do it by His Spirit. The yielded members of the Body of Christ are the tools in His hands on earth, bringing His plan to fruition. If this were not the case, the entirety of the story He is telling would lose meaning.

As promised, all enemies will be under foot. We learn that our adversary, the devil, will be thrown into the lake of fire (Revelation 20:10). Satan will not exist in heaven, but the Lord wants to be with a people that freely chose Him when other options existed. He wants to be with a people who are "in His own image," co-heirs who loved Him on earth and invited His Spirit to lead them during their pilgrimage in a fallen land.

It is the leadership of His Spirit that will ultimately accomplish His final work. He will guide His people to conquer and reign. It has always been His desire to have a people who would listen and obey so they could accomplish His good purpose on the earth to vanquish the works of the adversary.

God's Kingdom is not like the kingdoms of this earth. His plans of conquest are not like the plans of men. They will certainly come to pass.

"God is not human, that he should lie, not a human being, that he should change his mind. Does he speak and then not act? Does he promise and not fulfill?" (Numbers 23:19)

When His Kingdom manifested on earth, its advance came with the death of the very King Himself. He loved not His life unto death. This was extreme obedience.

As His ambassadors, we are called to the same level of obedience. We are to surrender to our commander's agenda. As we learn to abandon ourselves to His purposes, we have many great and wondrous promises to fill us with hope. We will go from glory to glory, all the while eagerly anticipating the return of our King in the fullness of His Kingdom.

CHAPTER 3:
Joshua, the Trail-Blazing Conqueror

Growing up, I always loved movies that showed hints of the end from the beginning. When the end was revealed, I would always react with the same "I knew it!" Most of the time that was a false claim, but something inside picked up on the clues and exploded with excitement with their onscreen fulfillment. The moment all the clues were unlocked and everything came together, the world seemed good and right. Although I didn't recognize it at the time, God's story of redemption and the restoration of all things was written on my heart. As these scenes unfolded, my heart was crying out in agreement.

One of my favorites begins when Andy Dufresne arrives at the Shawshank prison at the beginning of the movie *Shawshank Redemption*. Andy is on a life sentence for a crime he didn't commit. Upon arrival, Warden Norton gives all his new inmates a copy of the Bible and tells them, "Salvation lies within."

The warden plays the part of the enemy a little too well. Seeing the introduction to evil start with the Bible is all too appropriate. Religion has been a powerful tool for the power hungry for way too long. As the film progresses and evil appears to have prevailed, we see the culmination of all things. When all seems hopeless and any normal viewer would presume Andy is ready to end his life, he escapes! The device? The same Bible the warden used as a tool for evil has become a tool that brings Andy his freedom.

We learn Andy had slowly dug through a concrete wall over a 20-year period with a small rock hammer. The hammer was kept hidden inside the Book of Exodus in the Bible! When the warden discovers the hollowed-out Bible in his safe, he also finds an inscription from Andy: "Dear Warden, You were right. Salvation lay within."

GOD'S USE OF FORESHADOWING

As we read the Bible, we begin to see a pattern of God showing us His own love of foreshadowing. He is, in fact, the author of foreshadowing. Sometimes He outright tells a thing through a prophet—other times, He hides it within a story.

"It is the glory of God to conceal a matter; to search out a matter is the glory of kings." (Proverbs 25:2)

Uncovering a mystery is a glorious thing, and we find God celebrates this game of hide and seek. Heaven shall never be boring because He is endless, so I envision an environment of endless discovery of the one who is endless. Sounds a lot more interesting than playing a harp on a cloud to me!

Back to God's use of story in foreshadowing a greater story He is, in fact, telling. The principle or pattern is a type of lesser fulfillment in the beginning, followed by increasingly greater or complete fulfillment of the larger story being told later. Some people simplify this as "first to one, then to many." This trend plays out throughout scripture unto this day. We yet see some of the greatest promises in the Bible fulfilled. The result is a struggle for context for the fulfillments to come.

We make our best guesses. How will God do the thing He promised? We write books, give sermons and even make movies about such topics, based on our conjecture. Our need is clear. We want to know what goes down and how it goes down! We desperately want to conceptualize God's plans! Perhaps the clues are in the stories themselves? I believe they are.

If the religious folks of Jesus's time would have known God and understood His ways, perhaps they wouldn't have missed it? He would have led them to the mysteries revealed in His Law and opened up His secrets. He loves to hide the end of a matter within a lesser story, but without knowing Him, the story is simply a parable. Relationship unlocks the mystery. They would have seen and recognized Jesus as the Messiah, but their relationship was with the rules and not God. The same possibility holds true for us today.

Jesus fulfilled every previous type, pattern, and associated timing required by the Law and prophets, but His method messed them up. They got tripped up by looking beyond our Savior's requirement to first come as the sacrificial servant and lamb, and instead focused on the end of the matter. In prioritizing His ultimate role as King of heaven and the earth, they misidentified salvation and missed the other components of His story.

The Passover story was a well-told example. The slaughter of the lamb at the original Passover was a critical part of their culture and heritage. The remembrance of coming under its blood was celebrated annually by the inhabitants of Judea and beyond. And though the feast of Passover also marked the Israelites crossing into the Promised Land 40 years after their exodus from Egypt, an even greater fulfillment still remained.

Sacrificed on the day of Passover roughly 1,500 years after the exodus, Jesus was the fulfillment of the blood of the perfect lamb. In coming under the blood of Jesus, we are freed from the slave master of the law and its requirements and are seen as just in the eyes of God. The requirement of the law was justice, and the sacrifice of the perfect lamb was the only thing that could meet God's just requirement. This was all, however, lost on the majority of Judeans.

Although an animal could temporarily meet the need, according to the Law, such a one-time sacrifice could never provide the necessary justice to cover all sins for all time for those under that sacrifice. Thus, we see a type or "shadow" with God's instruction and miraculous provision that inaugurated the exodus from Egypt. This shadow is repeated annually to commemorate the event, but also even in the daily sacrifices by the priests. He drilled the point home through the Law and prophets, illustrated it continually in their practices…and they still missed the fact that it was simply a shadow!

The Passover was only one example. The story of Jesus was on display in the life of Joseph, whose brothers betrayed him for a bag of silver so God could prepare a way for them all. We could tell the story of Jesus in Boaz, Moses, Daniel and many others who point us to both His first and second comings. Yet with all of those examples, the majority of the scribes and scholars missed it! Let us heed the warning. We are vulnerable to the same fate of only having a relationship with the rules or clinging to traditions rather than knowing Him.

What, then, is He saying? What mysteries would He have us know so we are aware? Through the Scriptures, we see a pattern. We see it in specific events like feast days and the lives of His people. We see it in places and even animals. It is also on display in objects like the manna and the snake Moses lifted up for healing.

To focus on one of these examples, let's examine the lesser and greater fulfillment pattern in the feast of Pentecost. The original Pentecost was represented by the giving of the Law to the Israelites in the wilderness. The Law was given by God, but since it was not written on their hearts at that time, the Israelites lacked the ability to obey and, as a result, languished in sin and unbelief for another 1,500 years.

DEATH IN THE OLD MEANS LIFE IN THE NEW

Digging a little deeper, the original Pentecost and "post-Law" era was inaugurated by 3,000 of the Israelites being struck down in the wilderness for participating in the worship of the golden calf Aaron constructed. In the fulfillment of Pentecost after the resurrection, we see a new pattern develop. The Spirit was poured out on those gathered in the upper room in Jerusalem and just as 3,000 souls were struck down for worshiping the golden calf at the original Pentecost, 3,000 souls were added at this later fulfillment!

We discover that which produced death in the old covenant produces life in the new! This is fabulous news, news that requires an entirely new wineskin to carry and comprehend. Old thinking can no longer apply.

An additional example of death in the old becoming life in the new is found in Jacob's prophetic blessing of his lastborn son Benjamin, "the son of my right hand." Jacob, as the father and progenitor of all the tribes of Israel, prophesied over his sons futures on his deathbed. During this time Jacob declared Benjamin would be a "ravenous wolf." This later plays out as the tribe's actions almost get them extinguished from Israel in Judges 20 (they were reduced to just 600 men after the battle with their brothers).

The ravenous behavior of Benjamin is further developed in the life of King Saul, who relentlessly pursues David. In the New Testament, however, we see Jacob's prophesy come into a radically positive light. Galilee was a Benjaminite area and it is believed most of the Apostles were from this tribe. We also learn that Saul, from the tribe of Benjamin, who starts off ravenously persecuting the early church, is converted to radically bring life to the church!

We find that God chose to use the wolves, the underdogs, to advance the Kingdom after His atoning sacrifice. After all, He is the one that caused what once meant death to become life. He established this concept as a prophetic and directional pattern to guide our expectations of the full redemption to come. With the perfect sacrifice now in place, we can expect God's redemptive plan to apply to all until He "becomes all in all."

God did not create us to destroy us, He created us to redeem and restore us. To enjoy His plan, we must first be justified by His blood and sanctified by the fire of His Spirit before we can be glorified as He was at His resurrection. Perhaps, just perhaps, we aren't all on the same time schedule in this beautiful pre-ordained chain of events? Some are ahead, called to be the overcomers who display His ways to the world, while some need more surrender and training on His ways.

Understanding these concepts is important as we study the life of Joshua. As a prophetic shadow of a generation to come (first to one, then to many), he led Israel to an unprecedented rout of the enemy inhabitants in the Promised Land. If we also use the principal of what was death in the old becomes life in the new, we begin to see a picture of what will happen spiritually when the Joshuas of the earth are awakened. To summarize the story and cut to the chase, the enemy will be completely routed and multitudes will come to life!

JOSHUA'S PROPHETIC NAMES

As we begin to look into the life of Joshua for what is to come, we will start with his name. Like most of the types and patterns, the greatest prophetic fulfillment in Joshua's life is that of Jesus. Unlike the others, these two share the same Hebrew name: יְהוֹשֻׁעַ (Yehoshu'a), meaning "YAHWEH is salvation." However, in Numbers 13 when Moses selects twelve men to enter the Promised Land, we learn that Joshua's name was actually the result of a name change. Moses changed his name from Hoshea to Yehoshu'a. His original name Hoshea simply means "salvation." Moses made an addition, inserting God's name into Joshua's (like Abram becoming Abraham). Prophetic name changes in Hebrew were to add "Ya" or "Ha" to represent God's name.

We see that Joshua gets a prophetic addition to his already prophetic name. This is all to show through whom God's salvation was supposed to come. Let us first focus on the prophetic nature of Joshua's original name Hoshea, since this is often overlooked and the name is a signpost for Israel's destiny.

First, King Hoshea was the last king of the northern tribes of Israel before they were taken captive by the Assyrians in 722 BC. At the time, Israel was a divided nation with a northern kingdom

(10 tribes) and much smaller southern kingdom (2 tribes). King Hoshea was the king of the significantly larger northern kingdom. This massive group of Israelites encompassed millions of people and along with King Hoshea was overthrown and carried away, to fulfill prophecy.

After this absolutely critical event in Israel's history, the Old Testament scriptures shift to focus on the remaining two tribes, who the prophets call Judah (although comprised of Judah, Benjamin, and some Levites). The remaining prophets and books of the Old Testament track the Babylonian exile of these two tribes and their return to the land. Jesus was to come through Judah, so all of this was necessary to fulfill prophecy.

Although the storyline shifts, God does not lose track of His people. This is made clearly evident the next time the Hebrew name meaning "salvation" appears. This occurs with one of King Hoshea's contemporaries, the prophet "Hosea." Although missing the "h" in the translation of his name, we see the same Hebrew meaning of "salvation." Most date Hosea's prophecies to the time period just before and during the captivities of the northern tribes. Again, God was using a name to foretell the story of would come to pass.

First, God has the prophet Hosea marry a prostitute named Gomer, then he provides him with the names for their children. Jezreel means "God scatters," or "God sows." Lo-ruhamah means "no mercy." Lo-ammi means "not my people." God was going to scatter the people of Israel and "sow" them into the earth like seed. He was going to show no mercy with the displacement of His beloved people for their harlotry, going as far as removing their identity among the nations so they would no longer be remembered as His people.

This has certainly happened. However, like unsuspecting viewers of Andy Dufresne's preparation for escape before it occurs in *Shawshank*, there is little to no discussion about Israel in this context. God does not mind—His plan has always been redemption and He loves hiding a matter so His kings can search it out. Thankfully, unlike in film, He does not leave us guessing about the eventual outcome! He even provides the end of the matter right within the story.

"I will plant her for myself in the land; I will show my love to the one I called 'Not my loved one.' I will say to those called 'Not my people,' 'You are my people'; and they will say, 'You are my God.'" (Hosea 2:23)

God used another nation to judge His people for prostituting themselves with other gods, then we see His ultimate plan was to restore them. It is important to note these people are not of Judah, so they have never been called "Jews." The term Jew actually does not appear until after the Babylonian captivity, a good 200 years after God sent away His people.

To summarize Hosea, God was to send off and sow millions of His children into the earth, only to later reclaim them. In the Christian world, we know them as "the lost tribes of Israel," but God calls them "my people." These ten tribes carry the name "Israel" and God Himself was never going to lose track of them.

IDENTITY OF THE NATIONS

Why did these tribes carry the name Israel and not the two southern tribes? The name pertains to birthright and causes us to go back even a little further in Joshua's story and heritage. It is a worthwhile journey, as we must see how it fits into the larger story God is telling.

We learn that Joshua is of the tribe of Ephraim, son of Jacob's "Israel"-beloved son named Joseph. After the betrayal at the hands of his brothers causes years of hardship, Joseph forgives them and restores unity in the family. God ultimately used Joseph's story for the "salvation" of Israel. Salvation simply means to save, and in this story Joseph saved his family from the famine in Canaan. As with Jesus, this salvation required forgiveness. Rather than choosing bitterness in his reunion with his brothers, Joseph chose to focus on what the Lord had done in reuniting them.

"You intended to harm me, but God intended it for good to accomplish what is now being done, the saving of many lives." (Genesis 50:20)

The entirety of Joseph's story is so important nearly 25% of the book of Genesis is surprisingly about him. After the reunion his brothers, we also learn that Joseph was the recipient of the birthright of his father Jacob.

In our birthright sequence we have Abraham, who left his father's house to go on a journey with God to an unknown territory and received the promises. Isaac, Abraham's promised son through Sarah at her old age. Jacob, who worked by deception to gain the birthright from his brother Esau, and now Joseph, who we will learn receives that same birthright before his father Jacob's death.

To learn more about the birthright itself, we see God's original promises to his great grandpa Abraham.

"I will surely bless you and make your descendants as numerous as the stars in the sky and as the sand on the seashore. Your descendants will take possession of the cities of their enemies, and through your offspring all nations on earth will be blessed, because you have obeyed me." (Genesis 22:17-18)

This promise came after God had already established with Abraham:

"I will establish my covenant as an everlasting covenant between me and you and your descendants after you for the generations to come, to be your God and the God of your descendants after you. The whole land of Canaan, where you now reside as a foreigner, I will give as an everlasting possession to you and your descendants after you; and I will be their God." (Genesis 17:7-8)

As birthrights work, all of these promises fell on Joseph when Jacob blessed him. This birthright, originally given to Adam at creation, renewed through Abraham and spoken personally by God to Jacob himself, was in fact passed on in a "double portion" fashion to Joseph's sons.

"Jacob said to Joseph, 'God Almighty appeared to me at Luz in the land of Canaan, and there he blessed me and said to me, 'I am going to make you fruitful and increase your numbers. I will make you a community of peoples, and I will give this land as an everlasting possession to your descendants after you.

"'Now then, your two sons born to you in Egypt before I came to you here will be reckoned as mine; Ephraim and Manasseh will be mine...' Then Israel said, 'Bring them to me so I may bless them... May the God before whom my fathers Abraham and Isaac walked faithfully, the God who has been my shepherd all my life to this day, the Angel who has delivered me from all harm may he bless these boys. May they be called by my name and the names of my fathers Abraham and Isaac, and may they increase greatly on the earth.'" (Genesis 48:3-16)

In this account, it is clear that Jacob claimed Joseph's sons Ephraim and Manasseh as his own and gave them his name. It's equally interesting to note that Ephraim's name means "fruitfulness" and Manasseh's name means "causing to forget." Their names speak prophetically to the destiny of their descendants. They were to become fruitful in the earth, fulfilling the promises made to their forefathers, yet their identity as God's own would be lost.

This Genesis account isn't just for Joseph's sons. It records Jacob's last words to all of the sons (tribes). He didn't give this blessing to any others. Thus, when we later learn Joshua is of the seed of Joseph through Ephraim and his name means "salvation," we pay attention. When we discover Moses (of the priestly line of Levi) adds God's name to that name to make it "God is my salvation," we should come out of our seats. God is speaking loudly! What is He saying? "Pay attention! I'm telling a story!"

This brings us to Joshua's role as a representative of Christ. What was he representative of? Jesus' life on earth does not seem congruent with Joshua's, so let's then focus on His second coming.

In leading the conquest of the Promised Land, Joshua claimed his birthright as the seed of Joseph. The land and the promises belonged to his tribe. Moses did not lead them in because Moses was not of Joseph. God is a legalist, He is bound to His Law. He gave the promises to Joshua's forefather, so the land belonged to his family. It was only Joseph's descendant's to conquer and divide among his brothers. This was all accomplished in the life of Joshua.

As we discover the beauty and confidence of Joshua's life, we learn he did not operate from "blind faith," rather a firm foundation of truth. Joshua approached the Promised Land with bold assurance because He knew God was faithful to His Word.

One example as a nation was the Israelites' stop along the way to collect Joseph's bones, to bury them in the land of his inheritance upon arrival. Upon exiting Egypt on God's wings, they knew their destiny was that land so they carefully collected the bones in faith. When Israel's confidence waned during the journey, it required the faith of a man on whom the promises rested to carry the nation into that destiny.

JESUS, COMING TO CLAIM HIS INHERITANCE

Why must we go into such detail to establish these points? So we can have the confidence of Joshua! When we understand that God is bound by His own Law and we read the countless promises in the Bible about our destiny, we can have this same confidence. Faith is required in the maker of a promise. "Blind faith" is not faith at all. Rather, trust in His Word, His track record, and His plan to provide a clear vision of our destiny, rather than blindness.

We can rest assured that "every knee will bow!" We can additionally rest assured that "His glory will cover the earth as the waters cover the sea!" These things will happen—so, like picking up bones to bury in a land you've never seen, we can speak life to the dry bones in front of us. Those dry bones will one day be bent in submission to Jesus. So why must we wait for that day? "The entire creation is groaning for the sons of God to be revealed" (Romans 8:19) in this manner. Ordinary men and women who move in great boldness and assurance of God's plans.

It is this supreme confidence in God and His plans that will mark His overcomers. Like Joshua, this group will be used of God as a bridge from the partial fulfillment of the promises of God to our full inheritance. This bridge will span a generation that will bring great change to the earth as we know it.

Although Jesus' death and resurrection reconciled all things back under the King's rule, we do not yet see all things under His feet. His first coming was about being a suffering servant, so the greater work is expected. If the life of Joshua gives us clues for what to expect, then we have a part to play.

"...and since that time he waits for his enemies to be made his footstool." (Hebrews 10:13)

CHAPTER 4:
Joshua's Prophetic Life

In 1812 a boy was born in Portsmouth, UK who had no observable chance in life. His father's debts were piled so high his entire family lived in a debtor's prison with no hope of recovery. The boy's family would toil long hours in a locked workhouse year after year to pay back their debts. Even once the debts were cleared, hopes of climbing outside the poverty class in Victorian England were dim.

In spite of the long odds this young man turned into quite the worker. Strengthened by a positive attitude and lighthearted disposition, Charles Dickens would overcome the odds to write literary classics Great Expectations, Oliver Twist and more. Dickens perhaps recalled his humble beginnings as he wrote words that are still quoted today. "It was the best of times, it was the worst of times" so well describes the epic journeys of the greats.

The journey of Joshua is no exception to that of the greats. His character was honed by a challenging start. Although we don't see him significantly on the scene until he is anointed by Moses to lead Israel into the land, we know he certainly endured suffering. After observing the beauty of the Promised Land during his 40 day tour and having the faith to enter in, he had to endure 38 years of waiting. Although he would one day lead the children of the faithless generation in, he would have to face them daily and remember what could have been. This must have been grueling. A deeper look at Joshua's story will help us understand why he made the most of his opportunity when it finally came.

EARLY INDICATIONS OF A CALLING

When we first encounter Joshua, as with Hebrew tradition, he is always referred to in the context of his father. Joshua was the son of Nun. We are not told much about Nun, but every time I read his name I think about Joshua being the son of "none." Although an extrapolation, it was as if the Lord had made him a son of "none" or no man, so he could be a son of God.

Why is this important? Just as we know that all of creation eagerly awaits the revealing of the sons of God, not elevating an earthly man as our example eliminates the ceiling on our potential. Limits, for whatever reason, have been placed on us and being a son of God means removing those limits to take the risk He is calling us to. This is the story of Joshua.

The first time we learn about him is when he is mentioned in the context of a battle against Amalek at Rephidim. At nearly 40 years old, Joshua was chosen by Moses to lead the Israelites in what became a rout. Amalek was a descendant of Esau and many believed they were giants. The word Amalek in Arabic is Al-'Amālīq, which actually means "giants." Why is this important? Just as David had faced the lion and the bear while shepherding before facing Goliath, Joshua had already faced giants before he encountered them in the Promised Land.

The next time we see Joshua, as we previously visited, he is selected as one of the twelve to spy out the Promised Land. Let's look at the story to see the goal of the mission.

"When Moses sent them to explore Canaan, he said, "Go up through the Negev and on into the hill country. See what the land is like and whether the people who live there are strong or weak, few or many. What kind of land do they live in? Is it good or bad? What kind of towns do they live in? Are they unwalled or fortified? How is the soil? Is it fertile or poor?

Are there trees in it or not? Do your best to bring back some of the fruit of the land." (Numbers 13:17-20)

Earlier we saw Joshua and Caleb's warning to the children of Israel not to rebel, here is their initial report upon return.

"We went into the land to which you sent us, and it does flow with milk and honey! Here is its fruit. But the people who live there are powerful, and the cities are fortified and very large. We even saw descendants of Anak there. The Amalekites live in the Negev; the Hittites, Jebusites and Amorites live in the hill country; and the Canaanites live near the sea and along the Jordan." (Numbers 13:27-29)

Ten of the spies came back and reported that the land looked awesome, BUT that they had no chance of conquering it. Remember they feared the large inhabitants and daunting cities that lie in the land God had promised them. To them, it was a hopeless cause. Caleb had a different take. He and Joshua were ready to go. Caleb spoke for them both and said that they should go take the land. Armed with all the experiences with the Lord in leaving Egypt and the conquest over the giants of Amalek, Joshua and Caleb knew the Lord was faithful to come through regardless of how things appeared.

However, the other ten spies sowed fear into the people, being led by what they saw with their eyes and perceived with their minds. In the natural, the Israelites had no shot. Eventually, so much fear entered the camp, the people wanted to turn back to the land of slavery from which they came. They even devised a plan to overthrow Moses and appoint a new leader to take them back to Egypt! We have all personally seen and experienced this happening in our own lives when we see only with our eyes and perceive only with our minds. Without the Spirit, we are just like these people.

As a result, the Lord was so angry Moses had to plead with Him not to destroy the people. Thoughts about this exchange could fill a book in itself, but knowing His Law and trusting His character, I think Moses had something on God in this one. Moses knew God had made an unconditional covenant with Abraham to bless him through Isaac and again made the promise to Jacob. These were those descendants. So although in one interpretation it could appear Moses had to talk God out of destroying His people, the story rather displays God's frustration about their level of maturity at this point (like a parent of a teenager!) God had nurtured the people, but they simply were not ready. In fact, here we are, 3,500 years later and perhaps only just getting ready to handle what God wants to pour out on us.

Moving on, amidst what almost appeared to be destruction for Israel, the Lord made a promise about the ultimate destiny for all of creation. This promise was also repeated 1,000 years later by the prophet Habakkuk. And just as Moses held God to His own Law in this exchange, we can do the same with the promise that follows (and is further established by Habakkuk to provide a second witness).

"The Lord replied, "I have forgiven them, as you asked. Nevertheless, as surely as I live all the earth shall be filled with the glory of the LORD." (Numbers 14:20-21)

"For the earth shall be filled with the knowledge of the glory of the LORD, as the waters cover the sea." (Habakkuk 2:14)

The Lord, outside of time, uses this moment to make a declaration about the earth's ultimate destiny. To be like heaven, to be filled with His glory. Habakkuk, speaking for the Lord, provides the double witness. Want evidence God's ways are not ours? He just performed signs and wonders, parted a sea, fed this grumbling people, and brought them straight to the land He promised them! After all of that, they say "no thanks."

God does not use the moment to destroy them. Instead He tells Moses, his friend, how the story ends! Are you kidding me? Maybe we should take notes for our personal journey when somebody betrays us? Point to the scoreboard of your heart and say, "Oh yeah, this thing ends amazingly regardless!" Being His friend, God also gives Moses more detail in this moment.

"But your assistant, Joshua son of Nun, will enter it. Encourage him, because he will lead Israel to inherit it." (Deuteronomy 1:38)

Friends give friends details, and this was an important one. He wanted Moses to know Joshua would need years of encouragement and preparation for the coming task.

SEPARATION OF THE OVERCOMERS

Even though Joshua was selected, we know that sin has its consequences. None of the children of Israel would survive to see the land except the men of faith, Joshua and Caleb. But because of Israel's sin, even these two would have to wait another 39 years to inherit the promise. It took that long for the faithless generation to die and the new generation to arise.

When the time arose, although both had the faith in God's promises, Caleb was not chosen to lead God's people into the land. The explanation is simple. He was of Judah and not Ephraim (Joseph). The land was Joseph's to inherit, so Joshua was the one to lead them in and ultimately divide up the land.

This is a good time to step back and observe the similarities between Joshua in this moment and those of us of the Joshua Generation. We have been armed with the promises, the assurance of victory, and the sufficiency of the sacrifice that reconciled all things back under the rule of the King. Do you see where this thing is headed? Why in the world would we be like the generation that heard the report of a defeated enemy and want to go back to Egypt? As obvious as the answer may seem, without knowing and fully trusting Jesus, we will be like that faithless generation.

"But we do not belong to those who shrink back and are destroyed, but to those who have faith and are saved." (Hebrews 10:39)

This indeed is true of the overcomers, those of the Joshua Generation that are rising on the earth to put all things under the King's feet by loving as He loved.

Continuing with the story of Joshua is his commissioning by the Lord through Moses before his death (more on this in a later chapter).

"So the Lord said to Moses, 'Take Joshua son of Nun, a man in whom is the spirit of leadership, and lay your hand on him...' Moses did as the Lord commanded him. He took Joshua and had him stand before Eleazar the priest and the whole assembly. Then he laid his hands on him and commissioned him, as the Lord instructed through Moses." (Numbers 27:18,22-23)

The Lord had Moses do this in front of the people so they would follow Joshua's lead. Remembering the principle of what brought death in the old brings life in the new, we see the importance of this commissioning. When Joshuas are commissioned of the Lord, believe His promises, and are led by His voice, the people will be drawn in. Why? Because the Spirit of the Lord brings life. Those sent by the Lord will be like springs of living water throughout the earth. The people will be drawn to learn about the Lord and be refreshed!

Unlike the first Joshua, whose inheritance came to an end, the scriptures make clear there will be no end to the Joshua Generation that is rising. This brings to mind another principle from the scriptures, the principle that displays the temporary nature of types and shadows to point to the eternal nature of their fulfillment. The conquest of the Promised Land was never designed to last. In fact, before Moses died the Lord had him do an interesting thing. He gave him a song to sing in front of the children of Israel. The song was about their ultimate destiny as a nation. This song, found in Deuteronomy 32, foretells their turning to foreign gods in the land and the Lord casting them off.

One benefit to being friends with God is He gives you the inside scoop! Just like He told Abraham that His descendants would be slaves to a foreign country, God told Moses the fate of His people.

It's not all bad news, however, because we know our God is all about redemption. The song ends with redemption: "he will...make atonement for his land and people" (Deuteronomy 32:43).

Immediately after the death of Moses, we see the transfer of power. The significance of this is found in the previously established biblical concept we established earlier of "first to one, then to many." And the mantle of Moses fell on Joshua.

"Now Joshua son of Nun <u>was filled with the spirit of wisdom</u> because Moses had laid his hands on him. So the Israelites listened to him and did what the Lord had commanded Moses." (Deuteronomy 34:9)

How does this apply to us?

"Truly I tell you, among those born of women there has not risen anyone greater than John the Baptist; yet whoever is least in the kingdom of heaven is greater than he." (Matthew 11:11)

It does not take much extrapolation to conclude that John the Baptist was greater than Joshua, and thus, we in Christ (in the Kingdom) have received a greater mantle than he. Joshua received his at the passing of Moses, while we received ours at the passing of One greater than Moses. Therefore, we must be mindful of the words of our King: "...from the one who has been entrusted with much, much more will be asked" (Luke 12:48).

THE CALLING

Joshua was commissioned by God to bring the entire generation of Israelites into the Promised Land, rout the enemy God had used to prepare the land, and divide the inheritance with God's people. When he starts to speak directly with the Lord in Joshua 1, God's words to Joshua are reminiscent of Jesus' words that speak to us today.

"No one will be able to stand against you all the days of your life. As I was with Moses, so I will be with you; I will never leave you nor forsake you." (Joshua 1:5)

Jesus repeats these words for us, compiling two verses from Matthew we get the following: "...I will build my church, and the gates of hell will not overcome it. And surely, I am with you always, to the very end of the age" (Matthew 16:18, 28:20).

The Lord has never changed. Jesus Christ is the same yesterday and today and forever (Hebrews 13:18). Even with the taking of the Promised Land by Joshua and this generation, we will explore the victory of Christ at the cross and the down-payment of the Spirit provided at Pentecost, and we have yet to see all things placed under His feet. The world still appears broken, many presume Satan is in power, and God appears slack concerning His promises. As we continue with the Lord's initial words to Joshua, we will see how they are the message for today's Joshua Generation. These words provide a message that causes us to arise and claim the land.

"<u>Be strong and courageous</u>, because you will lead these people to inherit the land I swore to their ancestors to give them. <u>Be strong and very courageous</u>. Be careful to obey all the law my servant Moses gave you; do not turn from it to the right or to the left, that you may be successful wherever you go." (Joshua 1:6-7)

Thank God Joshua was filled with the Spirit of wisdom as we discovered earlier! If not, he wouldn't have been empowered to follow these commands. But when the Spirit of the Lord fills us, we follow His commands because they are written on our hearts. Like Joshua, we can accept His directive to be strong and courageous...so we can be successful wherever we go!

Many Christians today spend their time speaking about and incessantly praying against a defeated foe. Meanwhile, when the Spirit has done His work in our lives, we are enabled to not turn from His Law "to the right or to the left." And **we know that anyone born of God does not continue to sin...and the evil one cannot harm them** (1 John 5:18). That's a promise that empowers us to step out in boldness and without fear. Indeed, we can be strong and very courageous.

Let's continue our God's truth, considering it like a coach's pep talk, perhaps the best in the history of motivational entreaties!

"Keep this Book of the Law always on your lips; meditate on it day and night, so that you may be careful to do everything written in it. Then you will be prosperous and successful. Have I not commanded you? <u>Be strong and courageous.</u> <u>Do not be afraid; do not be discouraged</u>, for the Lord your God will be with you wherever you go." (Joshua 1:8-9)

With this, the Lord ends His initial conversation with Joshua. In the last four verses, the Lord *encourages* Joshua to be courageous five times! The first three times he says it outright, the final two he tells him not to do the opposite. Do not be afraid means "be fearless" (courageous), and do not be discouraged means "be courageous!" The key? "Keep this Book of the Law always on your lips." The Lord promises Joshua if he follows His instructions, he will be prosperous and successful! Then God closes this amazing send-off by once again promising Joshua He will always be with him.

Let me restate: as His overcomers, the Lord has made this same exact appeal to us today. Jesus said all of these words and made these promises to all "who have ears to hear." Then why have we languished so long? Just as the great awakenings and revivals did not occur until 1,500 years after Christ's resurrection and the original outpouring of the Spirit, I believe ears and hearts are only now being awakened to the brilliance of our true identity in Him.

Joshua mobilizes the people, and the people answer the call.

"Then they answered Joshua, "Whatever you have commanded us we will do, and wherever you send us we will go...just as we fully obeyed Moses, so we will obey you...Only be <u>strong and courageous</u>!" (Joshua 1:16-18)

Now I do not believe the people heard the Lord speaking with Joshua, rather God chooses to speak through the people back to

Joshua once again. The message? You got it: Be strong and courageous! If the Lord gives you a message six times, you know you are going to need it. And Joshua did.

STEPPING OUT IN FAITH

This time, Joshua sends two spies into the land, to the city of Jericho. God makes a way for them through the hospitality of Rahab the prostitute. Let me suggest God is a bit different from the religious types of our day! The two spies return with this report.

"The Lord has surely given the whole land into our hands; all the people are melting in fear because of us." (Joshua 2:24)

Let this contrast of realities shine its bright light in our hearts. Joshua is strengthened by the Word of the Lord to take courage, while the fear is so evident in the enemy these spies *know* the land has been given to them. This must have been some seriously tangible fear. I don't know exactly what the spies witnessed, but wet pants and puddles of urine come to mind!

God's people then proceed across the Jordan as the Lord miraculously cuts off the flow of the river, allowing them to pass on dry land. Let's just say this miracle brings some credibility to Joshua's ministry.

"That day the Lord exalted Joshua in the sight of all Israel; and they stood in awe of him all the days of his life, just as they had stood in awe of Moses." (Joshua 4:14)

In yet another way, the life of Joshua speaks to the generation that is now arising on the earth. Jesus turned water into wine, walked on water and raised the dead, yet promised that "whoever believes in me will do the works I have been doing, and they will do even greater things than these" (John 14:12). Jesus used these works to glorify His Father and so will the Joshuas, who are the first fruits of creation and called to be like Him. In the words of Jesus and

John, "when a student is fully trained he will be like his teacher" (Luke 6:40), and "but we know that when Christ appears, we shall be like him, for we shall see him as he is" (1 John 3:2).

After this miracle, Joshua learned sometimes the process of obedience can be painful. The principal of cutting off of the old so the new can come forth was established when God blessed Abraham at the age of 99 and gave him the covenant of circumcision. It is not only interesting Joshua had to next lead the children of Israel into this covenant before inhabiting the Promised Land, but necessary.

Just as "you cannot put new wine into old wineskins" (Matthew 9:17), circumcision spoke to the cutting off of the old life so the new can come forth. This was absolutely necessary in this symbolic crossing over. With a looming battle in Jericho ahead, it was not for physical pre-battle preparation, rather, it was a spiritual sign for the generations! In the same way, Joshuas of this generation will spearhead the heart circumcision of many.

SO THAT ALL WOULD BE SAVED

What happens next is simply awesome, revelatory and instructive.

"Now when Joshua was near Jericho, he looked up and saw a man standing in front of him with a drawn sword in his hand. Joshua went up to him and asked, 'Are you for us or for our enemies?' 'Neither,' he replied, 'but as commander of the army of the Lord I have now come.' Then Joshua fell facedown to the ground in reverence, and asked him, 'What message does my Lord have for his servant?' The commander of the Lord's army replied, 'Take off your sandals, for the place where you are standing is holy.' And Joshua did so." (Joshua 5:13-15)

Now this "commander of the Lord's army" is the Lord. We know this because the ground becomes Holy with His presence. What is most interesting is His answer to Joshua's question about who He is for: "Neither" Israel, nor the enemy! Really!? This simple answer is mind-blowing. I mean, aren't God's people, the good guys, rolling in there to destroy the bad guys?

Apparently, the Lord doesn't see it this way. He is neutral when it comes to sides. We learn more about God's heart on this matter with Jonah and the Assyrians, Saul and the Gibeonites and many other apparent "enemies" of Israel whom the Lord then shows that He loves, honors and even protects.

The broader principal we learn here is that without understanding the context of the larger story, we simply live in a smaller story. Without understanding that God loves *all* His people and chose to work His plan for salvation and redemption for them *all* through a family, we lose context.

God chose His people so He could first come into a family Himself, then initiate a new family of faith that would manifest Him to the entire world. He tells the story through this family as the ultimate "first to one, then to many." This is a demonstration of the destiny of His creation. This is marvelous news!

When we start to look at the necessity of battles, the conquests of nations, and the death of millions, we must maintain context. In the case of the Lord appearing to Joshua before the battle of Jericho to declare He is for neither of them, He is making an emphatic statement that there is a larger story unfolding.

The Lord then personally gave Joshua what appears to be instructions that are unorthodox. If He is this detailed, then we must trust there is a deeper meaning. We will explore the deeper meaning behind these instructions in a later chapter focusing on the Feast of Tabernacles. For our focus on Joshua, the Lord went ahead and Joshua and his chosen men executed the plans and took the city.

We can follow Joshua's formula. Meet with the Lord, get the battle plans and follow them. Kingdom conquest is sure to follow. Upon victory at Jericho, Joshua pronounced a prophetic oath, which was initially stated as a curse on anyone who rebuilt the city of Jericho. Like most of scripture, this oath contains a much deeper meaning.

"At the cost of his firstborn son he will lay its foundations; at the cost of his youngest he will set up its gates." (Joshua 6:26)

We know the Lord gave His "only" Son, so this Son was to be both the firstborn who lays the foundations of the heavenly Jerusalem and the lastborn who sets up its gates because He is one and the same! After this oath we learn what happens when the Lord is with you.

THE TEMPTATION OF PRIDE

"So the Lord was with Joshua, and his fame spread throughout the land." (Joshua 6:27)

Without a new wineskin and the character of the Lord, fame, even granted of God, can bring ruin. The thief so easily enters into the pride gate because it is what brought his own fall. In His rebuke to the "King of Tyre" through the prophet Ezekiel, God paints a picture of Satan that provides guidance for the ones He lifts up.

"You were the seal of perfection, full of wisdom and perfect in beauty. You were in Eden...every precious stone adorned you...Your settings and mountings were made of gold; on the day you were created they were prepared. You were anointed as a guardian cherub...You were blameless in your ways from the day you were created till wickedness was found in you...Your heart became proud on account of your beauty, and you corrupted your wisdom because of your splendor. So I threw you to the earth...So I made a fire come out from you...you have come to a horrible end and will be no more." (Ezekiel 28:12-19)

There is so much information in this text! We learn this fallen one received his splendor from God and had a great start, even being identified as "blameless." We also learn he was in the garden with this splendor, perhaps explaining why glorious Eve could be so allured and tempted by him. But then we find out the seal of perfection, the wisdom and the beauty God gave him caused pride to arise. This pride led to his downfall. He fell so far God "made a fire come out from" him. In other words, he became a useful tool in God's hands to judge and train the nations. Ultimately, once his usefulness has been used up, we learn that he "will be no more."

This detail on what appears to be Satan is for the benefit of our understanding. God is the giver of wisdom, beauty, splendor, and success. Receiving such gifts can cause the extremes of pride and humility. When we are selected as Joshua was, it should cause a deep humility like we saw in Jesus, Joshua, Moses, David, and many others the Lord lifted up in the eyes of men. Israel is our picture, and as with Israel, He did not choose us because of us. Although He has fully equipped us, He chose us as a foolish thing so that His name would be made great so none of us can boast.

"The Lord did not set his affection on you and choose you because you were more numerous than other peoples, for you were the fewest of all peoples." (Deuteronomy 7:7)

This is all mentioned because, in the old wineskin, pride has too often been the case in the body of Christ. This shall not be the case with the overcomers that are arising. The Joshua Generation will be known for their humility. They will live out Jesus' words that "anyone who wants to be first must be the very last, and the servant of all" (Mark 9:35).

OVERCOMING SIN IN THE CAMP

After the victory at Jericho, confidence was brimming. They were so confident in fact, the spies returned from Ai saying it would only take a few thousand men to take that city. Their confidence sank quickly, however, after their mission failed and the Israelites were routed at Ai. It was revealed that "sin was in the camp." The sin of one led to the loss of many.

Achan, a man in the camp allowed his desire for riches to directly violate the Lord's instructions concerning the sacred treasures in Jericho. Israel temporarily lost her favor as a result and Joshua fell down before the ark of the Lord (he did not seek Him before the first battle with Ai, so the loss could have been avoided). The Lord's response?

"Stand up! What are you doing down on your face? Israel has sinned…That is why the Israelites cannot stand against their enemies; they turn their backs and run because they have been made liable to destruction. I will not be with you anymore unless you destroy whatever among you is devoted to destruction." (Joshua 7:10-12)

The Lord promised blessing and victory while Israel was on the path. However, leaving the path has consequences. The Lord's favor was not on them, so they lost. After identifying the perpetrator, Joshua addresses the issue immediately.

"Then Joshua said to Achan, 'My son, give glory to the Lord, the God of Israel, and honor him. Tell me what you have done; do not hide it from me.' Achan replied, 'It is true! I have sinned against the Lord, the God of Israel…When I saw in the plunder…I coveted and took them…' Joshua, together with all Israel, took Achan son of Zerah, the silver, the robe, the gold bar, his sons and daughters, his cattle, donkeys and sheep, his tent and all that he had…Then all Israel stoned him…Then the Lord turned from his fierce anger." (Joshua 7:13-26)

Let's again apply the principle of "death in the old has become life in the new." Joshua took care of the matter at hand. Sin was in the camp and it had to be dealt with before God's blessings and provision again could flow. The same is true today—however, rather than killing the Achans of today, Joshuas will restore them in love. If the Achan, having given his life to Christ already (as to be an Israelite), desires to remain in sin, we are instructed to hand "this man over to Satan for the destruction of the flesh, so that his spirit may be saved on the day of the Lord" (1 Corinthians 5:5).

Harsh? We have to remember the Lord never changes. Although His atoning sacrifice means restoration for all things, if we don't use its power to restore, our brothers and sisters will continue to be routed by the enemy. And if we allow those to remain among us who have no desire to be restored, how can we expect God's blessing and provision to flow? Let's restore those who desire restoration and allow those who don't to step away from the fellowship until Satan has again reminded them why we need Jesus!

Since the Lord turned from His anger, victory ensued. After the victory, I believe Joshua remembered the Lord's original instruction to "be careful to obey all the Law...so you will be prosperous and successful." To ensure what happened with Achan didn't happen again after Ai, Joshua did his part.

"Joshua read all the words of the Law, the blessings and the curses just as it is written... There was not a word of all that Moses had commanded that Joshua did not read to the whole assembly of Israel, including the women and children, and the foreigners who lived among them." (Joshua 8:34-35)

PERFORMING UNPRECEDENTED MIRACLES

Joshua's next battle was with five Amorite kings in Chapter 10. Before the battle the Lord assured Joshua victory, so as Israel was in hot pursuit and losing daylight, Joshua commanded the unthinkable to the Lord in the presence of His people.

"'Sun, stand still over Gibeon, and you, moon, over the Valley of Aijalon.' So the sun stood still, and the moon stopped, till the nation avenged itself on its enemies." (Joshua 10:12-13)

He told the sun to stand still in the sky! If you want to disciple a generation in the ways of the Lord, this type of faith will help! There is a rich lesson for us here. If we have limits on our life, we cannot believe God for something like this. It goes against all science, logic, and reason, so how do we even conceive such a thing? We cannot, but He can. And what we pre-conceive will oppose our hearing.

When we ask a question of the Lord, how can we hear if we have come with our preconceived idea? Only in coming to Him in complete surrender and without limits can we hear a word like this! "John, I want you to go down to that morgue and raise all the dead." "But I was merely asking what we should do today, Lord!"

Let's remember He always has better plans for us, if we set aside our agenda when we ask. This is how the overcomers, the Joshua Generation, will approach this relationship. From a deep sense of identity, they will come to expect the unexplainable.

Joshua knew who he was, who He is and what both of their inheritance was to be. The land and the people were destined for this time. Joshua was chosen as a warrior and the inheritance belonged to his tribe. The Lord chose and prepared him for such a time as this. He was known for courage and trusted the Lord's promises fully. The two characteristics that go hand in hand, courage and trust in the Lord marked his life.

After Joshua led the conquest of the five kings, he led the Israelites to victories over 24 more kings. Joshua led conquests of 31 kings in total. He grew old and at the end of his life there was still land left to be taken. The task was left for a future generation. This future generation of Joshuas have waited for their appointed time. Their assignment is to finish the mission of putting all things under His feet. To help lead a nation of God's people into their destiny.

FINISHING WELL

Even with land left to be taken, God gave Joshua the honor of dividing the inheritance. After giving instructions to each tribe on their allotted portion, Joshua called an assembly of the leaders and said his farewells. Even in his final days, Joshua remained a man of truth. He used the moment to strengthen and warn them about their future. The prophesy was rooted in God's Law, echoing God's original instructions to him.

"Be very strong; be careful to obey all that is written in the Book of the Law of Moses, without turning aside to the right or to the left...One of you routs a thousand, because the Lord your God fights for you, just as he promised. So be very careful to love the Lord your God...You know with all your heart and soul that not one of all the good promises the Lord your God gave you has failed...But just as all the good things the Lord your God has promised you have come to you, so he will bring on you all the evil things he has threatened, until the Lord your God has destroyed you from this good land he has given you. If you violate the covenant of the Lord your God, which he commanded you, and go and serve other gods and bow down to them, the Lord's anger will burn against you, and you will quickly perish from the good land he has given you." (Joshua 23:6-16)

Eventually these warnings would become reality for Israel. Although the nation would reach its height in Solomon's day, the wisest man who ever lived would violate his own covenant with the Lord and turn to idols. The resulting curses meant the territory of Joshua's victories would be lost. The kingdom was split after Solomon's reign, eventually resulting in mostly idolatrous kings. This brings us back to Joshua's original prophetic name: Hoshea. Joshua's warnings and resulting violations would one day culminate with Israel's final King Hoshea while the prophet Hosea would tell God's side of the story.

After speaking these things, Joshua's prophetic life would end in very prophetic fashion. He renewed their covenant at Shechem.

Shechem is the first place Abram stopped in the Promised Land and built an altar after the Lord promised him the land. Jacob later built an altar here after buying the land. This is also the place where the bones of their birthright holder, Joseph, were laid. Additionally, the name Shechem was later changed to Sychar, which brings us to another significant connection.

"Now he had to go through Samaria. So he came to a town in Samaria called Sychar, near the plot of ground Jacob had given to his son Joseph." (John 4:5-6)

Here is Jesus later at the very same place as we learn Jacob gave this land to Joseph. The connections are significance and endless, because these glimpses display depth and texture to how perfect and detailed the Lord is. So Joshua's renewing of the covenant happens at Shechem. A place that will become Israel's first capital (before Bethel and Jerusalem).

In renewing the covenant, the Lord reminds them of all the ways He provided for them. And Joshua warned them yet again. After the people assured Joshua they would follow the Lord, we see Joshua's final action.

"On that day Joshua made a covenant for the people, and there at Shechem he reaffirmed for them decrees and laws...Then he took a large stone and set it up there under the oak near the holy place of the Lord. 'See!' he said to all the people. 'This stone will be a witness against us. It has heard all the words the Lord has said to us. It will be a witness against you if you are untrue to your God.'" (Joshua 24:25-27)

In his final days, Joshua did all he could to prevent the inevitable. You get the sense he knew the people would rebel and that God would enact the curses attached the covenant. He knew the Lord always honored His Word. We are now in a time with more and greater promises available. The Joshuas appointed for this time will stand on God's unconditional promise that "all the earth will be filled with His glory." Like Joshua, their hearts will be fixed on the promise and not what their eyes see and their minds interpret. Because of the greater promises now available, their faith will ignite a Kingdom wildfire on the earth that will not be quenched.

We have explored Joshua's prophetic name, his conquering life, and the promises that still remain. As we add more context to what has transpired since Joshua's time, we will be able to openly explore what living a life like Joshua's would look like today.

CHAPTER 5:
Realizing our Destiny

In the late 1940's a young believer from Portland, OR named Jim Elliot got a burning desire to share the gospel of Jesus with a people who hadn't heard it. After meeting a missionary to Ecuador and hearing the story of the Huaorani, also called the "Auca" (native word for "savage") Elliot's heart was stirred. This group of Ecuadorian indigenous people were considered violent and dangerous to outsiders, but Jim was undeterred.

After years of planning and some delays, finally at the age of 24 Elliot and his friend Pete Fleming from Washington arrived in Ecuador. Shortly after their arrival they moved to the jungle and began training to reach the Huaorani. During that time Jim married his college sweetheart and even had had a daughter while staying at a mission station.

After almost four years of preparation, Elliot and four other missionaries that included his friend Pete finally made contact with the Huaorani. Using a loudspeaker and a basket to pass down gifts from their airplane, the small team made progress with the natives.

After several months, the men decided to build a base a short distance from the village to work on establishing trust and contact with the natives. After becoming friendly with a small group of Huaorani they even gave an airplane ride to one whom they called "George". Encouraged by their friendly encounters, they made plans to visit the main village, not knowing their new friend went back and lied to his people about the missionaries' intentions.

Unsuspecting and still planning their visit to the village, one day ten Huaorani warriors attacked and killed Elliot and his four companions. Later it was learned his journal entry from seven years before expressed his belief that work dedicated to Jesus was more important than his life. "He is no fool who gives what he cannot keep to gain that which he cannot lose."

After Elliot's death, Life magazine published a ten-page article on Elliot and his friends' and a generation of new missionaries became inspired. Even the Huaorani would eventually be reached by Jim's wife Elisabeth and a brave team that would continue their work with the dangerous native Indian tribe.

There is an appointed time for us all to realize our destiny. Jim Elliot had the valor of 13th century Scottish liberator William Wallace, who is credited with saying "every man dies, not every man really lives." Both heeded their call and activated the very substance of things unseen. They bravely stepped into the journey God marked out for them. As we press on to further fathom God's ways, we learn that even He has appointed times. Not only for His people, but for all of creation.

FULFILLMENT OF THE APPOINTED TIMES

As we established earlier, some plans on the journey to fullness have seen their ultimate fulfillment, while others are yet to be realized. There will not be another sacrificial lamb to fulfill Passover, since that was completed in Jesus. The same is true with Pentecost. The Law was given on the first Pentecost at Sinai and its fulfillment came 1,500 years later when the 120 gathered in the upper room after Jesus ascended. The Spirit of the Law came to dwell in man to fulfill Pentecost.

Passover and Pentecost represented two of the feast days for Israel. All of the men were to present themselves before the Lord three times each year, however. This means we are yet to see the fulfillment of the final feast, the fall feast of Tabernacles.

Occurring during the largest harvest season, the feast of Tabernacles also goes by the names of the Festival of Ingathering, Booths, and Sukkot. Following the solemn Day of Atonement,

Tabernacles was to be a time of great celebration. Although the Lord gave clear instructions for it, it was rarely celebrated by the children of Israel, with one great exception. The exception came when the glory of the Lord filled Solomon's Temple one the last day of the Feast. 120 priests blew their trumpets and something unprecedented occurred.

"When Solomon finished praying, fire came down from heaven and consumed the burnt offering and the sacrifices, and the glory of the Lord filled the temple. The priests could not enter the temple of the Lord because the glory of the Lord filled it. When all the Israelites saw the fire coming down and the glory of the Lord above the temple, they knelt on the pavement with their faces to the ground, and they worshiped and gave thanks to the Lord, saying, 'He is good; his love endures forever.' Then the king and all the people offered sacrifices before the Lord." (2 Chronicles 2:1-4)

The most extravagant temple ever built was filled with the glory of the Lord during the Feast of Tabernacles. The most extravagant offering (142,000 animals) ever provided by man to the Lord also occurred on this same day. We see the Lord's response.

"I have chosen and consecrated this temple so that my Name may be there forever. My eyes and my heart will always be there." (2 Chronicles 2:17)

THE COVENANT WITH SOLOMON

This was His desire, but He could not reside forever with sin. Just a few verses later, He lays out the conditions of this covenant with Solomon.

"But if you turn away and forsake the decrees and commands I have given you and go off to serve other gods and worship them, then I will uproot Israel from my land, which I have given them, and will reject this temple I have consecrated for

my Name...this temple will become a heap of rubble." (2 Chronicles 7:19-21)

Thus ensues the destiny of both Israel and the temple. In fact, this very moment commemorates the height of Israel's empire. A little more than 1,000 years later, after the Holy Spirit is poured out on the 120 gathered in the upper room at Pentecost, Peter stands up to connect the dots for us.

"However, the Most High does not live in houses made by human hands. As the prophet says: 'Heaven is my throne, and the earth is my footstool. What kind of house will you build for me? says the Lord. Or where will my resting place be? Has not my hand made all these things?'" (Acts 7:47-50)

All the effort Solomon and Israel put into building the Lord a house was to provide us with a type and shadow! He never wanted to dwell in a house made with hands! What then are the clues from the original filling of the temple we can then pull from to gain insight? The timing: Tabernacles. The nature: extravagant sacrifices, amazing glory. The backdrop: awe and worship.

SUDDEN VICTORY

As we press into better understanding the Feast of Tabernacles, we get another fulfillment picture with Joshua's first conquest. This conquest set up all the rest. The depiction is a week-long event marked by celebration, sacrifice, a tabernacle of the Lord, and sudden complete victory.

"The seven priests carrying the seven trumpets went forward, marching before the ark of the Lord and blowing the trumpets. The armed men went ahead of them and the rear guard followed the ark of the Lord, while the trumpets kept sounding. So on the second day they marched around the city once and returned to the camp. They did this for six days. On the seventh day, they got up at daybreak and marched around the city seven times in the same manner, except that on that

day they circled the city seven times. The seventh time around, when the priests sounded the trumpet blast, Joshua commanded the army, 'Shout! For the Lord has given you the city! The city and all that is in it are to be devoted to the Lord.'" (Joshua 6:13-17)

This is our destiny. Death in the old means life in the new. Taking the city in a sudden victory, won by the Lord through men, is symbolic of our destiny. These depictions are the types and shadows. The fuller picture awaits. If we have learned from Passover and Pentecost, we know the ultimate fulfillment is always way better than our minds can conceive. When is this to happen? Only He knows, but we have the promises.

"The Lord is not slow in keeping his promise, as some understand slowness. Instead he is patient with you, not wanting anyone to perish, but everyone to come to repentance." (2 Peter 3:9)

The Lord is long-suffering in waiting for all things to be put under His feet. He is patient in training His own to step into their inheritance and claim what belongs to Him. He was patient in waiting for the next generation of Israelites to be ready for Joshua's time and He has not changed. The prophetic pattern established in Joshua's time points to a generation that will also cross over.

In what sequence can we expect these things to unfold? The first fruits (also referred to here as conquerors or overcomers) are our focus. Paul clearly shows the first fruits are raised before His return.

THE FIRST RESURRECTION

"But each in turn: Christ, the first fruits; then, when He comes, those who belong to him." (1 Corinthians 15:23)

Paul makes it clear to state "then." It refers to His coming. The first fruits Paul mentions above are raised first. These are the overcomers we call the Joshua Generation. We believe Paul was also a type of Joshua, demonstrating a life like that of Jesus along with an enduring hope of being transformed into His glory.

"I want to know Christ—yes, to know the power of his resurrection and participation in his sufferings, becoming like him in his death, and so, somehow, attaining to the resurrection from the dead. Not that I have already obtained all this, or have already arrived at my goal, but I press on..." (Philippians 3:10-12)

When Jesus returns, we know that Paul says when we see him, we will be like him. Jesus comes back for conquest, but in his perfect way. He does not choose to do this on his own, rather he chooses to raise up his overcomers for the first resurrection to assist him.

Paul's first letter to the Corinthians, this declaration continues and culminates:

"I declare to you, brothers and sisters, that flesh and blood cannot inherit the kingdom of God, nor does the perishable inherit the imperishable. Listen, I tell you a mystery: We will not all sleep, but we will all be changed— in a flash, in the twinkling of an eye, at the last trumpet. For the trumpet will sound, the dead will be raised imperishable, and we will be changed. For the perishable must clothe itself with the imperishable, and the mortal with immortality. When the perishable has been clothed with the imperishable, and the mortal with immortality, then the saying that is written will come true: 'Death has been swallowed up in victory.'" (1 Corinthians 15:50-54)

We could go on extensively about eternal rewards and striving to participate in the first resurrection, but all of this would be to establish this point: How we live our lives matters. Did we learn to love? Are we forgivers? Do our hearts burn for what His burns for? These things are only activated as we love and trust Jesus so much that we surrender fully to Him and allow His Spirit to do its full work in our lives. These are the marks of the Joshua

Generation, the marks of those who will do great exploits before and after the redemption of our bodies.

In the scriptures, we see a pattern of 12 being God's perfect government. There are 12 tribes of Israel, 12 apostles, 12 foundations to the new Jerusalem, 24 elders which we know is 12+12, and the list goes on. I was recently called in on jury duty, and, thankfully, it was the first time I've been into a court of law. I say thankfully, because usually it's not a place you want to be! As the judge stated "you are the judges, I am merely the referee of the law," I felt the father say "exactly."

I was drawn to the words of Jesus when he said "I came not to judge you." The law does a mighty fine job of that in itself. I have come to see that the overcomers are simply administrators of His perfect Law. With the work on the earth to teach and train the people his ways.

Going back to our pattern of what is death in the old becomes life in the new, light is shed on the life of Joshua we reviewed. He conquered the lands by destroying the people therein. Conquerors of the new covenant, filled with His Spirit, will administer Jesus's ways perfectly to a world that will be put under His perfect rule.

This Joshua Generation will rise on the earth and be empowered by the fullness of his spirit as a fulfillment of the third and final feast. We know that we have seen the greater fulfillment of the feast of Passover (unleavened bread) and the feast of Pentecost, so we must anticipate with great expectation the fulfillment of the Feast of Tabernacles, a time of the first resurrection when we will be made to be like Him. It is the fullness of His Spirit that empowers us to for fulfill our Joshua calling.

The patterns have been given to us as signposts. Just as the scrolls of the Old Testament provided plenty for God's people to anticipate the Messiah's coming, we have more to bring clarity to His return. We have a fuller picture and the warning provided by the generation that missed it. Will we miss it now? Will our eyes be blinded to what now appears to be simple truths, the way theirs were? God forbid. If their blindness is a type and shadow of His second coming, we will benefit from heeding the warning. Jesus wants His bride ready.

"For in him all things were created: things in heaven and on earth, visible and invisible, whether thrones or powers or rulers or authorities; all things have been created through him and for him." (Colossians 1:16)

CHAPTER 6:
Rising to our Calling

In the late 13th century a man of lesser nobility was born into a nation falling into deep bondage. He would grow up seeing his people subjected to increasing servitude at the hands of a ruthless king. The king was Edward I of England, also known as Edward "Longshanks". The common man was William Wallace of Scotland, whose bravery was recognized in our last chapter.

As young William was growing up, he watched on as King Alexander III of his native Scotland died and Margaret of Norway also died en route to becoming Alexander's successor. Edward I seized the opportunity and advanced on Scotland during this leadership void. Edward mocked and taunted the successor Scotland would finally name for the throne.

As fear and bitterness swept the land, Wallace's appointed time was at hand. Assembling a small band of rebels, Wallace and his crew won unprecedented victories over the much larger English forces. With each battle the rebels won, the confidence of the nation grew.

Eventually Wallace and his partner Andrew Moray would earn the title Guardians of the Kingdom of Scotland for their work. As faith arose among the commoners of Scotland, Wallace would eventually pay a steep price for rising to the call for his nation.

After being captured in 1305, William Wallace was taken to the Tower of London. He was stripped naked and dragged through the city at the heels of a horse, hanged, and drawn and quartered. After being released from the noose still alive, he was emasculated, eviscerated and his bowels were burned before him before his ultimate beheading. Edward then had him cut into four parts and placed his head on a pike atop London Bridge.

I share these gruesome details because they mattered to the sons of Scotland. Much like our King, Wallace's suffering would not be in vain. Within fifteen years of the resistance led by Wallace, the people of Scotland would reclaim their freedom.

William Wallace was a type of deliverer in the likeness of Moses, Joshua and eventually Jesus. With a similar backdrop to what young Wallace witnessed in Scotland, God is raising another generation of deliverers for his people. In laying down their lives for the true King, this generation will be heeding the call of the Spirit from deep within.

Like Moses, who seeing his people in bondage, stepped into action at the age of 40. Although misguided in killing an Egyptian torturer, God saw someone He could use. Moses' determination to take action turned into forty years of training in the wilderness. When God finally appeared to him at the burning bush, Moses received the call. His time of training was concluding and the calling lodged deep within him was being activated by his Father. God is doing the same with our generation as we arise out of our own times of preparation.

Are you hearing the call from your Father?

EMPHASIS OF RADAH THROUGHOUT SCRIPTURE

Before His arrival on earth as Jesus to demonstrate the ways of the Kingdom, the Old Testament records the journey to His arrival. Like with every great story, this one is rich with foreshadowing. God has woven so much of it into the story, in fact, that we could study our entire lives and continuously discover more of His larger story in the small and seemingly insignificant ones.

One wonderful illustration of God's plan for our destiny is in the name of the family God would later come into, none other than Israel. The literal translation of this name from Hebrew is "Triumphant with God" or "who prevails with God." We see the theme connect again. God's plan, made clear at creation, was now on prominent display. His chosen family's name would literally mean "conquering with God!" Let us look at the story.

"After Jacob returned from Paddan Aram, God appeared to him again and blessed him. God said to him, 'Your name is Jacob, but you will no longer be called Jacob; your name will be Israel.' So he named him Israel.

"And God said to him, 'I am God Almighty; be fruitful and increase in number. A nation and a community of nations will come from you, and kings will be among your descendants. The land I gave to Abraham and Isaac I also give to you, and I will give this land to your descendants after you.'" (Genesis 35:9-12)

We saw this story earlier in a covenant context, but our focus here is to see God giving Jacob a new identity and the Adamic mandate. The mandate was to be fruitful and multiply. Jacob now had the birthright and promise previously given to his forefathers Isaac, Abraham, and originally Adam. He also inherited the unconditional promise God made to Abraham that his descendants would be as numerous as the stars of the sky and the sand of the seashore.

At the time of receiving his new name, however, Israel lacked the authority to fulfill the dominion mandate given to Adam. In order to bear God's image fully, God's own Spirit would need to reside in man.

Before we see God enter the story in a full human experience as Jesus, we have another *radah*, or dominion mandate, given to a man. This was given to another member of the family bearing the name of His plans. Right in the middle of human history (approx. 1,000 BC, which is about 3,000 years after Adam and 3,000 years before the present) and right in the middle of the Bible in Psalm 72, we find Israel at the height of its earthly empire. During this time, David writes a coronation Psalm for his son Solomon. We previously looked at how God would later fill Solomon's temple with His glory, but this was to recognize the role for the new King of Israel. It prophetically speaks to true fulfillment of the Kingdom under King Jesus.

"May he defend the afflicted among the people and save the children of the needy; may he crush the oppressor... May he rule from sea to sea and from the River to the ends of the earth... For he will deliver the needy who cry out, the afflicted who have no one to help. He will take pity on the weak and the needy and save the needy from death. He will rescue them from oppression and violence, for precious is their blood in his sight." (Psalms 72:4, 8, 12-14)

Here, in the context of the crowing of an earthly king, we get a description of ruling the Kingdom way. What does ruling look like in God's eyes? "May he have dominion [*radah*] from sea to sea..." Verses 4 and 12-14 then display what that dominion looks like: to bring redemption to the poor, to help heal the hurting, to crush the oppressor.

The conquering that God desires is clarified further as a type that protects the defenseless and provides justice to the oppressed. To exercise dominion over creation therefore means to honor and protect it.

Taking this back to the beginning, we get a beautiful picture of God's original intentions which have never changed. A paraphrase of our very original instructions in Genesis 1:28, expanding on Godly *radah*, would read: **"Be fruitful and have children, caring for My creation by filling the earth and conquering everything in it that leads to death. I am giving you the ultimate challenge to become like me and be an ambassador of my ways over the natural world, over the diversity of all My beautiful creatures."**

JESUS DEMONSTRATING RADAH

Like Jacob when he received his new name, neither Solomon nor Israel had the authority and resulting ability to have lasting dominion. After falling back into idolatry and unbelief under kings who set up kingdoms in their own images and images of this world, Israel was conquered. Only a small remnant of the people of Israel returned to and populated the land by the time of Jesus' arrival. The Law became religion and approximately 1,000 years after Solomon, we find Israel under subjection to the Roman kingdom. This is the backdrop for the Lord's fulfillment of His promise.

"The Spirit of the Lord is on me, because he has anointed me to proclaim good news to the poor. He has sent me to proclaim freedom for the prisoners and recovery of sight for the blind, to set the oppressed free." (Luke 4:18-19)

After waiting until the age of 30, and upon completion of 40 days of fasting and temptation in the wilderness, the Lord announced His royal entrance. He entered the temple to read the words that He gave the prophet Isaiah 700 years prior. The words described the type and nature of His rule.

This announcement was the earthly fulfillment of the promise to Adam and Eve. It was in complete alignment with His concept of *radah*, the same shared through the King and prophet David for his son Solomon in Psalm 72 after commencing his 40-year reign.

The religious leaders celebrated the memories of David and Solomon, but their lens for a kingdom was polluted by man's form of reign, most recently evidenced by how they were being ruled by the Romans. They lost God's concept of *radah* and tried to kill Jesus by throwing Him off a cliff right after this announcement.

This was the King announcing His entrance onto the stage, so the response was not a surprise. Two kingdoms were clashing. One would soon prevail with a permanent victory at the cross.

The Greek word for kingdom is *basileia*, which means royal power, kingship, dominion and rule. The gospel writers use the term 120 times. By contrast, the phrase "born again" is used only once. When you read the gospels with this in mind, you will find that nearly every parable Jesus told was about the Kingdom.

COMMISSION TO RADAH IN JESUS' FINAL WORDS

Jesus announced God's way of doing business, and He would have only a short time to train His co-heirs on how His Kingdom functions. With each parable, every teaching moment, interaction and miracle, He plays the role of a loving Father with His children—a King readying His princes for their eventual role as co-heirs.

Jesus acted as a chief architect, illustrating the blueprints to builders. The words were recorded (later becoming the Bible), and, like blueprints, provide a detailed plan for the builders to follow. If you have ever built before (particularly something that has never been built), you know how many questions you have when you review plans! Knowing this, Jesus made provisions. He promised and provided His Holy Spirit as foreman to ensure all the different pieces come together as planned. With the earthly demonstration finalized, the Lord gave His final instructions before sending the provision of His Spirit.

"And Jesus came up and spoke to them, saying, 'All authority has been given to Me in heaven and on earth. "Go therefore and make disciples of all the nations, baptizing them in the name of the Father and the Son and the Holy Spirit, teaching them to observe all that I commanded you; and lo, I am with you always, even to the end of the age.'" (Matthew 28:18-20)

Before Jesus ascended back into heaven, in the presence of His ambassadors, the Lord told them how *radah* will be accomplished. Consider this paraphrase: "Go make disciples of the entire earth, baptize them and teach them to do everything you saw Me do." It is the same mandate from God to Adam and Eve in Genesis 1, but now with a clear example to follow. William Wallace had lived his sacrificial life and was now entreating nation to do the same so to speak.

Informing people the King is here and teaching people His loving ways is what *radah* means. What was death in the Old Testament pointed to life, abundant life for all of creation. We needed to be informed and washed afresh to enter into this life, however. We would need to be taught and to teach and show others. The original mandate could finally be fulfilled! John the beloved disciple understood this.

That which was from the beginning, which we have heard, which we have seen with our eyes, which we have looked at and our hands have touched, this we proclaim concerning the Word of life. (1 John 1:1)

Only one thing was missing: Power. Just shortly after, on the day of Pentecost, Acts 2 records the outpouring of the Spirit on the King's ambassadors. The mandate, the demonstration, and the provision of power were all in place at last! God's people finally had the authority to conquer, to do their king's work.

GOD'S EMPOWERMENT FOR THE CHURCH

Years have passed since. Almost 2,000 of them. Each one has demonstrated the patience of the Lord. We have not sufficiently tapped into the power. We have yet to accomplish the task. The mandate to Adam with His first words to us in Genesis and final words before ascending remain unfulfilled. While a Promised Land across the Jordan still awaits, a bride is readying herself.

Though it may seem like a long amount of time to us, it has not been a surprise to Him. To assure us that His plan persists, He went ahead and gave us the book of Revelation. It proclaims that the plan of our glorious King will prevail, cementing the victory with tomorrow's headlines today. The bride finds her groom, and the adversary is finally defeated.

Does this book of the end, the revelation John received from Jesus Himself mention *radah*? The answer is a resounding yes! In fact, it provides the most dramatic evidence that God's plans never changed from Genesis 1 (4,000 BC), Psalm 72 (1,000 BC), Isaiah 61 (700 BC), and Jesus' ministry (30 AD), to the prophecies found in Revelation (70 AD - now).

The book of Revelation starts off with letters to each of the seven churches. Each of the letters ends with a promise "to him who overcomes." The word here being translated as overcomes is the Greek word *nikao* (to conquer, prevail, to carry off the victory, come off victorious, of Christ, victorious over all His foes). Is the connection clear? It is *radah*—right there at the end of each letter to each church! We will explore what these promises are for the conquerors in each of these churches found in Revelation Chapters 2 and 3:

- **Will "eat from the tree of life, which is in the midst of the Paradise of God."** (Revelation 2:7)

- **"Shall not be hurt by the second death."** (Revelation 2:11)

- **Will be given "some of the hidden manna to eat."** (Revelation 2:17)

- **Will be given "a white stone, and on the stone a new name written which no one knows except him who receives it."** (Revelation 2:17)

- **Will be given "power over the nations."** (Revelation 2:26)

- **"Shall be clothed in white garments."** (Revelation 3:5)

- **His name will not be blotted "from the Book of Life."** (Revelation 3:5)

- **His name will be confessed by Jesus "before My Father and before His angels."** (Revelation 3:5)

- **He will be given "A pillar in the temple of My God, and he shall go out no more."** (Revelation 3:12)

- **He will have written on him "the name of My God and the name of the city of My God, the New Jerusalem, which comes down out of heaven from My God."** (Revelation 3:12)

- **He will have written on him "My new name."** (Revelation 3:12)

- **He will be granted to "sit with Me on My throne, as I also overcame (conquered) and sat down with My Father on His throne."** (Revelation 3:21)

Are you ready to be tortured, ridiculed, made to look like a fool, surrender your life and go all in after reading these promises? Words cannot describe what is in store for us! These should create a hope so strong inside that it pushes us into our destiny.

We must behold the picture and hold fast to it. This is the story of our family. Paul states that he who is really of Israel is one who is inwardly, by the Spirit of God. The word translated as "Gentiles" is *ethnos*, which means "nations." When you believe, surrender your life to Jesus and receive His Spirit you become part of the family of nations united in Him.

We see God is making all the nations into one family, created to conquer the earth with Him. Need more evidence? Paul goes on to call us "co-heirs with Christ" (Romans 8:17), "more than conquerors" (Romans 8:37), and even says we "will judge angels" in (1 Corinthians 6:3). Paul wasn't alone. Peter calls us a "chosen people, a royal priesthood, a holy nation" (1 Peter 2:9), among many other examples in scripture detailing who we are and how God sees us. In Revelation 5:10, the Spirit confesses, "You have made them to be a kingdom and priests to serve our God, and they will reign on the earth."

Do we desire to conquer, but let old doctrines and confused beliefs hold us back? We must not let them! We will not spend long on this, but many popular Christian doctrines unwittingly hold to a theology of defeat, as if the enemy rules every "mountain of society" until Christ plucks us up to save us.

Sound familiar? What is the fruit produced by holding to this doctrine? It is the bad fruit of fear. A stench from the fruit rises from living "safe" lives devoid of Kingdom activity. It is far from what the early church believed. This recent doctrine appeared only in the last few centuries, popularized by editor's notes elevated to the level of scripture because of their placement in the widely-circulated Scofield Bible.

Yes, there will be persecution in the end, but that is because we are doing our part. Jesus said that we should anticipate it (John 16:33). It is a part of God's plan. God can use the enemy's push-back to His glory rather than our demise. The enemy's final desperate moves are from a defensive position, because he has already been defeated! Pin an opponent in a corner and you get a desperate response. Once the enemy's role to train God's people has been fulfilled, he is no longer useful!

So we have our mandate. We have our provision. We have our example. We even have our instructions. Furthermore, our Father provides us with the testimonies of the saints that have gone before us and stories of what worked and what did not work.

We have seen the bad forms of *radah* (the crusades, Inquisition, etc.) and we have the contrast of the martyrs' blood as the true "seed" of the church, poured into the soil and crying out like the blood of Abel.

We further have the documentation of the multiplication of the early church. Their unity in the Spirit fueled an explosion of radical Christians. But we have also seen Satan's response and the sharp contrast of the dark ages. Who would have thought after Pentecost, the Spirit could be relegated to a tiny lamp on a very dark planet?

What does all this church history speak to? Advance, retreat, or a mystery of God to be revealed in its proper time? As we dig into the symmetry of God's perfect redemptive plan and look into what has been hidden in plain sight in the law, we can peer into the fulfillment of our destiny within His Kingdom and His reward for those who conquer.

HISTORY OF THE CHURCH

The Greek word for church is *ecclesia*. It appears approximately 115 times in the New Testament. The Greek word *ecclesia* is defined as "The called-out ones," coming from *ecc* = out and *kaleo* = call. You can see how this word was used to indicate a body of selected people. Quoting from the Oxford Universal English Dictionary, *ecclesia*: "A regularly convoked assembly, especially the general assembly of Athenians. Later, the regular word for church."

Ecclesia was originally defined as a select civil body, summoned or convoked for a particular purpose. What, then, did the writers of the New Testament mean when they used the word *ecclesia* to describe a Christian body of people? It is reasonable to assume they were speaking of a body of Christians called out of the Roman and Judean systems to gather as a family and community under King Jesus.

Let's look at the earliest gatherings of called out ones. A body, a bride formed from His very side like Eve from Adam, born of the water and the blood. The fountainhead was the first outpouring of the Holy Spirit in Acts. The Spirit was the head and they functioned together in unity under His care and guidance:

"They devoted themselves to the apostles' teaching and to fellowship, to the breaking of bread and to prayer. Everyone was filled with awe at the many wonders and signs performed by the apostles. All the believers were together and had everything in common. They sold property and possessions to give to anyone who had need. Every day they continued to meet together in the temple courts. They broke bread in their homes and ate together with glad and sincere hearts, praising God and enjoying the favor of all the people. And the Lord added to their number daily those who were being saved." (Acts 2:42-47)

"'Now, Lord, consider their threats and enable your servants to speak your word with great boldness. Stretch out your hand to heal and perform signs and wonders through the name of your holy servant Jesus.' After they prayed, the place where they were meeting was shaken. And they were all filled with the Holy Spirit and spoke the word of God boldly. All the believers were one in heart and mind. No one claimed that any of their possessions was their own, but they shared everything they had. With great power the apostles continued to testify to the resurrection of the Lord Jesus. And God's grace was so powerfully at work in them all that there were no needy persons among them. For from time to time those who owned land or houses sold them, brought the money from the sales and put it at the apostles' feet, and it was distributed to anyone who had need." (Acts 4:29-35)

This is the birth of the Spirit in the body of believers. The seed in its original form birthed Christ's body as a collective. It serves as our example of *ecclesia*, a gathering of called out ones united in the Spirit. This is only found in God's Kingdom. No other assembling of people have experienced anything like this except for united members of His Kingdom.

This *ecclesia* is hardly more than a mustard seed in a massive garden at this point. In the context of the global population this is an ant to an elephant. However, what was happening was unlike anything in the history of mankind. Genuine freedom, signs, and wonders performed by ordinary people who forsook their personal riches to help others stunned onlookers. It was a growth that does not come from programs or evangelism techniques, but rather it was the Lord who "added to their number daily." It was a group of people who were so in love with their King and amazed at His power that they were magnetized. They could not help but accept his salvation and yield their lives to him.

This group was all-in. They were willing to do everything the King instructed. In fact, the Holy Spirit's presence created an environment so intoxicating they sold and shared all their possessions. Regardless of your political stance, you have to agree this was special. Observe what this account records about what the early church allowed the Holy Spirit to do among them:

1. Devoted themselves to the Apostles' teaching

2. Devoted themselves to fellowship

3. Devoted themselves to prayer

4. Devoted themselves to eating together

5. Were filled with awe at the signs and wonders performed by the Apostles

6. Praised God together

7. Enjoyed the favor of all the people

8. Went to temple (church) together

The result was that the Lord added to their number daily. This yielding to the Spirit caused their church to be a catalyst for the global growth of Christianity. Their unity in the Spirit fueled an unprecedented fearlessness among them.

BECOMING FEARLESS ONES

The Bible says to "fear not" 365 times. This level of fearlessness can only come from stepping into our resurrected life, knowing victory has been assured to us. Only then can our victory and breakthrough become someone else's victory and breakthrough. The rest of the world needs to see us.

"For the creation waits in eager expectation for the children of God to be revealed." (Romans 8:19)

There will be a generation when all of creation will see the sons of God operating in their fullness. There will be a first resurrection in which both Jesus and Paul speak to you. We should strive to be a part of this first resurrection—a time when we receive our eternal bodies like Jesus received his. He has the first of many brothers and his brothers are the sons of God. Joshua's faith is *an* example for us to follow. Jesus' victorious life is *the* example for us to follow.

The Book of Revelation shows us the end. Having your eyes fixed on the finish line can help with endurance during the race. Now is a time we need to look into the outcome of our faith so we can run with endurance. Revisit Revelation 12 with me:

"They triumphed over him by the blood of the Lamb and by the word of their testimony; they did not love their lives so much as to shrink from death." (Revelation 12:11)

The word for triumphed here? You got it. We *nikao*-ed the enemy. We conquered, overcame, arose victorious. This has already happened. How did we do it?

By the reality of what He accomplished on the cross and experiencing that personally in our lives. We became fearless because we awoke to the deepest reality of our identity.

We could only relate to the historical reality of His victory because of the personal reality of its impact on our own story. He stepped into our story, so our story became like His own. Just like the gospels were written about His life, we are living epistles. A victorious one. Amazing. Gospels could be written about His victory in our own lives. A testimony is simply the personal evidence that causes us to never again shrink back!

We see that our faith gets to an unshakable nature. Since it is written, just accept it as a historical reality like the resurrection. This grows our faith—as does hearing.

"Faith comes by hearing, and hearing by the Word of God." (Romans 10:17)

The word for hearing here is *rhema*. It is the spoken word. It is the same word Jesus used to rebuke the enemy during the temptation in the wilderness. The Word proceeding from the very mouth of God.

"It is written: 'Man shall not live on bread alone, but on every word that comes from the mouth of God.'" (Matthew 4:4)

Satan was talking about physical sustenance; Jesus was talking about real life. He was saying the spoken Word of God is the actual source of abundant life. The letter kills, but the *rhema* words bring life.

Even in the temptation scenario, Jesus wouldn't have been breaking the law by turning rocks into bread. There was no law producing a requirement for Him to fast for 40 days. Rather, Jesus was following the *rhema* instruction as the path to life. This brought victory over the enemy in this temptation and later at the cross.

Our faith comes from the spoken word. Then it becomes part of our history with God, our testimony, and then that's what we conquer with—his finished work and our own God story. We stand on those, our personal experience with him that confirms his work in our hearts.

With the living, spoken word guiding us, we can then stand as Joshua on the banks of the Jordan and get an accurate picture of the giants on the other side. Like the words flowing from God's mouth to our hearts, the giants must be bread for the journey. When we can stand on a promise, any obstacle in the way is simply for strengthening.

Let us not be like the Israelites who ignored God's promise and Joshua's good report. Rather, let us be a people who finally trust the good promise and interpret the obstacles with eyes of the Spirit rather than using our own understanding. Let us be the Joshua Generation arising on the earth for the great harvest at hand.

HEARING HIS VOICE

God uses the foolish things of the world to confound the wise (1 Cor 1:27). It's sort of His way to show people He is doing it. In fact, the more foolish, the better the story!

I love hearing these stories. I could listen to them all day. I recently realized the best testimonies I hear all have one thing in common: God's intervention. We often call this "hearing God's voice," but it's often not an audible voice. It's either a strong impression, another person delivering a message, a miracle or a combination of amazing things. In these people's lives a great adventure commonly follows. One of my favorites is the story of Prince Kaboo (Samuel Morris) of Liberia, Africa.

Born in 1873 as Prince Kaboo, Samuel was the son of the village chief. At 14, Kaboo was captured and tied to a post in the center of the village. After being beaten every day for weeks, one night there was a flash of light and a voice told Kaboo to run. His ropes fell off and his sick body gained strength. He ran into the jungle, wandered there for two weeks, and followed similar flashes of light. Eventually he arrived at a coffee plantation owned by a former slave who was a Christian.

The first week Kaboo was on the plantation, he attended church and heard the story of Saul's conversion to Paul. When the missionary shared about the "flash of light" Paul experienced, he jumped up and said "that happened to me!" He gave his life to Jesus and became a disciple.

As was common in the early church, one of the missionaries who became like a mother to Prince Kaboo, gave him a new name. The name she chose was the name of her financial sponsor from Indiana, Samuel Morris. She told him all she knew about the scriptures, but that was not enough for young Samuel. He was hungry for more! The only person the missionary knew who knew more was her teacher, a man in New York named Stephen Merritt.

Having never travelled more than his foot journey from the village, Samuel asked His Father about meeting Mr. Merritt. The next day he packed his bag and told the missionary, "my Father told me I am to go meet Mr. Merritt." She tried her best to talk him out of the journey, but young Samuel was determined.

As he walked to the shores of Liberia, Samuel prayed there would be a boat there to take him America. Sure enough, upon arrival he found a trading ship in port. God told Samuel the captain would take him to America, but when Samuel approached and asked the captain he was rejected and pushed to the ground. Later, when two of the crew members ran off, the captain was left short-handed and Samuel was allowed to board the ship in their place. It wasn't easy. He was bullied and beaten, but by the time their long journey to America concluded, Samuel had led over half the crew into a relationship with Jesus.

Upon exiting the ship in New York, Samuel asked the first hobo he saw if he would take him to Stephen Merritt. The hobo agreed to do it for $1. Samuel agreed and told the hobo, "my Father will pay you." In a city of millions, it turns out Samuel was with someone that actually knew Stephen Merritt from his visits to the 8th Street Mission.

Mr. Merritt was fascinated by the young man's story and paid the $1 fee, but he had to attend a prayer meeting that night so he asked Samuel to wait for him at his mission. When Mr. Merritt came back, he found Samuel in a prayer meeting of his own with the people of the mission. On his first night in America, he had led nearly twenty men to Christ. Impressed by Samuel's anointing and confidence, Mr. Merritt invited Samuel to stay at his house and later sent him to college. By the time he left New York for school, the young African boy who went to learn about the Holy Spirit had actually become the teacher.

While at Taylor University, Samuel was used by God mightily to draw people to the Lord. Students would stop by his dorm room to pray with him. People from around the world would come to hear him speak and to have him pray for them. He was known (and heard) to spend hours in prayer with God, from late at night to early in the morning. He inspired others to look at their relationship with God. Newspapers printed stories of the boy from

Africa who was charging Fort Wayne with the electric power of God.

When Samuel got sick and related to his fellow students that "my Father said it's time to go home," they resisted and prayed for his healing. But on May 12, 1893, at approximately 20 years of age, Prince Kaboo died. After his funeral, many of them said they felt led to go to Africa to be missionaries in Samuel's place. Though it was the custom in those days to bury blacks in the black section of the cemetery, Samuel's body was later moved to the center of the cemetery, linking blacks and whites in death like he did in life.

LEARNING DEPENDENCE

Becoming fearless requires a transition. We must go from worshipping the God of our understanding to knowing Him. As we do, He launches us into a new life by giving us a new identity. That new identity in Him leads us on a journey that requires faith and trust that can only come from relationship with Him. So we see a circle of dependence.

There are the people in authority along the way, like the captain of the ship, that do not initially recognize who we are, but as we radically trust our Father, they will bow their knee as well.

If we are as children and honor others like Samuel honored Mr. Merritt, God will use our foolishness to train the wise in our path. There will always be provision for our journey, even as God calls us on a new path. Eventually, he will send many to us like the students at Taylor University, so we can show them what real faith looks like. Where there is division, we will bring unity. We will one day be called home like Samuel was, and if we have followed our Father's voice, our homecoming will be cause for a great celebration.

As you listen to and journal with God, He will constantly reaffirm your identity in Him. We must get our identity from Him daily. In Him, we know who we are and from which place we pray. Jesus did not pray weak, whiny prayers, so neither should we. He prayed from the place of identity. When He stood before the crowd outside of Lazarus' tomb, He prayed:

"Father, I thank You that You hear Me. I knew that You always hear Me, but said this for a benefit of the people standing here, that they may believe You sent Me." (John 11:42)

Like Samuel, Jesus knew He was loved and pleased the Lord. When we pray from the place where He has filled us with His identity and authority, we start to pray the promises of our Father. Jesus said, "Do not believe me unless I do the works of my Father." I believe the Father is looking for us to say the same thing as we step out in the gifts, but it starts with allowing Him to build our identity. Then we can pray from the place of authority, knowing we are loved and bringing His will.

The Lord wants to work through us into all of the situations that make up our days on earth as we come out of the wilderness and into His Promised Land. In order for this to happen on a consistent basis, we need to tune to His station and hear His communication to us. As we do, we develop the relationship we will need to have an impact on the world around us.

We can talk about surrender all we want, but it's really a product of trust and relationship. Samuel's example is a great one for us. Perhaps we consider it easier because he had nothing and was on the brink of death, but we should consider our old selves as dead just the same. Everything from here forward with Christ is increase and adventure, because He loves us and we can trust Him. Samuel wasn't any different from us, He just had a genuine relationship built on trust and dependence. Deep inside that is all we want…and it is fully available. The narrow path is the path of relationship. The calling deep in our hearts is His voice, beckoning us to come away with Him and step into our destiny as one who has overcome this life.

CHAPTER 7:
A Joshua Heart

At 22 years of age the race of his life was upon him. After years of training and preparation, Eric Henry Liddell was now the favorite to win his specialty 100 meter race. As a representative of his native Great Britain at the 1924 Paris Olympics he was a shoe in to medal and bring honor to his nation. One problem arose, however. The race was to be held on a Sunday while Eric honored the Lord's day with rest.

Foreshadowing how he would live out the rest of his life in bold risk for the gospel, Eric chose to sit out the race. Instead, he ran a much longer race in the 400, for which he only had a few months to train. Before the race he received a folded piece of paper from a member of his team's support staff. Written on the paper was a reference to 1 Samuel 2:30 that read "In the old book it says: 'He that honours me I will honour.' Wishing you the best of success always." Eric ran that race and won the gold medal. He not only broke his personal record, but set a world record that would stand for 12 years.

Rather than choosing a life of fame in athletics that awaited him back home, Eric chose the dangerous mission fields of China. When asked about selecting a life of missions work over athletics, he said something that could have come from the mouth of Wallace, Elliot or even Kaboo. "It's natural for a chap to think over all that sometimes, but I'm glad I'm at the work I'm engaged in now. A fellow's life counts for far more at this than the other."

Like Elliot, Kaboo and many others before him, Eric Lidell would serve well and die young in the mission fields. After laboring exhaustively and still managing to inspire many alongside him in a Japanese internment camp during the war, he succumbed to a brain tumor at the age of 43. Liddell's story of living honorably, with heart and conviction, still inspires many today. He lived a life of sacrifice that was marked by joy.

In order to be the generation that enters the Promised Land, like Liddell, we need to recognize who and what is inside of us. The miraculous provision God has placed deep within. Recognition allows us to get practical and learn how to possess our vessels under His careful guidance. We acknowledge He is with us and for us. Together we dive deeper into the mystery of His plan and the beauty of His provision to help us accomplish our part in it.

In 1 Corinthians 3:16, Paul writes, "Do you not know that you yourselves are God's temple, and that God's Spirit dwells in you?" He goes on to state it again in Chapter 6. The concept was founded, way back in Genesis, when God breathed His Spirit Life into Adam at our conception, animating life into his body.

Earlier, we referenced Solomon's completion of the first temple in 2 Chronicles 7 when "the glory of the Lord filled the temple." Solomon had the best tradesman and finest materials the world had to offer. It took 20 years and thousands of men to complete it. To be sure, the temple was a really nice building. What made it a temple, however, was God's presence.

God's desire and intention has always been that we would be His temple, so He can dwell in us and have fellowship with us, but the church of the wilderness has made it about the buildings and formalities. Rather than intimate fellowship, we have implemented systems of hierarchy and manmade structures.

I believe the Lord cast His vote on these structures with the destruction of the temple in 70 AD. In Revelation, He states twice that he hates the doctrine of the Nicolaitans, which literally means "power over the lay people" (non-clergy in the church). He hates the structures we have built and by a move of His Spirit He will be tearing them down from within.

TEMPLES OF THE HOLY SPIRIT

When God's presence entered, everything changed. Adam probably had a very impressive-looking body, but it was lifeless before God breathed life into it. Similarly, the temple under Solomon was an example of what was to happen to each of us. We are designed for His glory to fill us. We are vessels. Containers designed to be filled with God's own Spirit.

"After this he went down to Capernaum with his mother and brothers and his disciples. There they stayed for a few days. When it was almost time for the Jewish Passover, Jesus went up to Jerusalem. In the temple courts he found people selling cattle, sheep and doves, and others sitting at tables exchanging money.

"So he made a whip out of cords, and drove all from the temple courts, both sheep and cattle; he scattered the coins of the money changers and overturned their tables. To those who sold doves he said, 'Get these out of here! Stop turning my Father's house into a market!' His disciples remembered that it is written: 'Zeal for your house will consume me.'

"The Jews then responded to him, 'What sign can you show us to prove your authority to do all this?' Jesus answered them, 'Destroy this temple, and I will raise it again in three days.' They replied, 'It has taken forty-six years to build this temple, and you are going to raise it in three days?' But the temple he had spoken of was his body. After he was raised from the dead, his disciples recalled what he had said. Then they believed the scripture and the words that Jesus had spoken." (John 2:12-22)

This passage is fascinating for a number of reasons, but a deeper question surfaces. Was Jesus zealous for the building and its courtyards? If the structures, why did He allow them to be completely destroyed in 70 A.D.?

God's valued currency is not a temple made with hands, as we read in Acts 7:48: "the Most High does not live in houses made by human hands." What, then, is a clear implication of this passage? When truly surrender your life to Jesus and welcome His Holy Spirit to do His work, He becomes a temple raider. He makes a whip and soundly whips every enemy inhabiting the space He was made to dwell in.

Here is the major caveat. In Revelation, He is addressing believers when He says, "Here I am! I stand at the door and knock" (Revelation 3:20). His desire is to come in, kick out our enemies, then sit down for a meal with us in His temple. This only happens to the extent we will allow Him to. He is a jealous God and He wants our vessels filled with Him. Will you let Him?

THE BATTLE FOR THE TEMPLE

"When the unclean spirit goes out of a man, it passes through waterless places seeking rest, and not finding any, it says, 'I will return to my house from which I came.' And when it comes, it finds it swept and put in order. Then it goes and takes along seven other spirits more evil than itself, and they go in and live there; and the last state of that man becomes worse than the first." (Luke 11:24-26)

Just like in life, in God's Kingdom there is a way things work. God has established the rules and boundaries and we have an enemy that, although forced to operate within them, impersonates God with the exact opposite agenda. He wants to come fill that same space! As we have established, our house/temple is designed to be filled. Here we see a clean house that does not get filled with the Spirit of God. What happens? This house becomes a ripe target to get filled nonetheless. Why? There are only two kingdoms. Both have the same agenda. The kingdom of darkness and the Kingdom of God both want access to the inside. In the unseen spiritual realm, people seem to be where the action is.

If you grew up in America, like me, it is probable you also spent countless hours unknowingly being influenced by a kingdom. If you were not saturated in an environment of God, it's likely you became synced up with the other kingdom…the kingdom of this world. Not so bad? John writes that "we know we are children of God, and that the whole world is under the control of the evil one" (1 John 5:19), and Paul reminds the Ephesians, "you used to live when you followed the ways of this world and of the ruler of the kingdom of the air, the spirit who is now at work in those who are disobedient" (Ephesians 2:2).

The kingdom of this world is, in fact, the kingdom of darkness. Now that God's Spirit lives in us, however, we are children of the Light. This fact (God's Spirit living in us) is the central dynamic of the New Testament and how the apostles and early believers lived the supernatural lives they did. If we are not being led by the Spirit, then how are we proceeding through life? By faith or by sight?

"For where your treasure is, there your heart will be also. The eye is the lamp of the body; so then if your eye is clear, your whole body will be full of light. But if your eye is bad, your whole body will be full of darkness. If then the light that is in you is darkness, how great is the darkness!" (Matthew 6:21-23)

The eye is a lens. Through it we see the world. Clear vision would be to see like Jesus and see: "what I see the Father doing." This is available to us when we walk in the Spirit. Most of us, however, accept Christ and even receive His Spirit, but still feel stuck.

"What do righteousness and wickedness have in common? Or what fellowship can light have with darkness?" (2 Corinthians 6:14)

The context here is Paul talking about being yoked with unbelievers, but does not it also apply to our own vessels as the fire of the Spirit sanctifies us? Our lens has been dirtied, and only through the Spirit can we learn to see clearly. Growing up in America, a foul power was powerfully at work in my eye gate and my ear gate. For countless hours from youth, I participated. With no actual intention, I willingly allowed a Trojan horse to be placed inside of me. An enemy plant, designed to build up internal defenses, so even if I said *the prayer*, Jesus could never really come in and set up His full tabernacle.

THE TROJAN HORSE IN THE TEMPLE

Here is a passage from Virgil's *Aeneid* on the Trojan Horse.

> *After many years have slipped by, the leaders of the Greeks, opposed by the Fates, and damaged by the war, build a horse of mountainous size, through Pallas's divine art, and weave planks of fir over its ribs: they pretend it's a votive offering: this rumour spreads. They secretly hide a picked body of men, chosen by lot, there, in the dark body, filling the belly and the huge cavernous insides with armed warriors.*

As the story goes, a Greek solider named Sinon accompanied the horse, telling the Trojans that the Horse was an offering to the goddess Athena, meant to atone for the previous desecration of her temple at Troy by the Greeks. This story was a little too close to the truth of growing up in America.

The sitcoms, the video games, the seemingly innocent movies, the news, hours upon hours of it all. We then spend our time talking about these shows and games and news, fighting about "our ideas." We never consider that our worldviews could simply be a compilation of the sum of what we've exposed ourselves to. Our temples have been polluted and our daily decisions can construct fences around the edifice.

America is not a communist country, but American's worldviews have been neatly packaged and presented in a myriad of creative ways in a strikingly similar fashion. Masquerading once again as an angel of light, the prince and power of the air offers us gifts to help us "pass the time." In time, our ideologies get deeply rooted. Without realizing it, we set the expectations for our lives based on what the planted horse speaks.

Our spouses have to look a certain way, we need to make a certain amount of money, certain life outcomes are considered a failure while others a success. We often find ourselves in one great "race to the middle" with our ideals. Have you ever noticed how TV shows are called "programming?" Hidden in plain sight is the effect of our exposure and willing participation...we become programmed.

What does God make of it all? Is all media "of the devil?" In the last chapter, we reviewed how different the Trojan horse looked during the Dark Ages. Christianity became the headline name of an institution that used control to perpetuate cycles of ignorance and illiteracy that fueled the leaders' power. The church and state were integrated as one and religion was the most effective tool in their hand. In this era, the Trojan horse placed inside the minds of people was that "God must rule this way."

Is it too bold to believe the powers of the darkness of this world have used the control of information to influence the minds of the populace? This has more recently played out in communist nations, but what about a "free" nation? This backdrop helps us understand why the Pilgrims persevered through so much hardship to come to a land where they could worship God freely.

It also helps us understand why freedom, freedom of religion most of all, was so important to our nation's forefathers.

HIDDEN IN MORSE CODE

This brings us to the story of Samuel Morse, who many call the father of modern communication, with his invention of the single wire telegraph. Morse was a very accomplished painter, and one day, while working on a piece he was commissioned for, a horse messenger delivered a letter from his father that read, "Your dear wife is convalescent." The next day he received a letter from his father detailing his wife's sudden death. Morse immediately left Washington for his home at New Haven, leaving the portrait unfinished. By the time he arrived, his wife had already been buried.

Heartbroken that for days he was unaware of his wife's failing health and her death, he decided to explore a means of rapid long distance communication. On May 24th 1844, Morse's passion became reality. In a demonstration witnessed by members of Congress, he dispatched a telegraph message from the U.S. Capitol to Alfred Vail at a railroad station in Baltimore, Maryland. The message "What Hath God Wrought?" was telegraphed back to the Capitol a moment later by Vail.

"For there is no enchantment against Jacob, no divination against Israel; now it shall be said of Jacob and Israel, 'What has God wrought!'" (Numbers 23:23)

The New Living Translation has the statement as "What wonders God has done for Israel!" In this beautifully prophetic moment, the world was thrust into a new era of communication. The history is fascinating. It turns out Morse had many powerful opponents. Why? I believe the enemy's initial reaction was fear. He was fearful about communication being used to spread the Truth.

When the Truth is revealed, so is the lie. Therefore, we have an enemy seeing communication potentially leading to his demise, so he aimed to shut it down. Morse tried to sell his technology to the U.S. government for only $100,000, but opponents on the inside rebuffed his offer. Eventually, however, using his age-old tactic of using God's innovation for his own device, the enemy saw opportunity. He could use the new technology for his purposes. The trend of God creating something and the enemy perverting it would thus continue, and the world would never be the same. Rather than overt control, this time he would have even deeper access into the temple of man. All he needed was willing partners for his scheme.

THE MEDIA MACHINE

Morse's simple invention opened up a gateway. An expansion of media so significant ensued that the average child now spends 53 hours a week staring at a screen. Games, shows, Facebook, Google and Instagram now fill our days. The consensus of the messaging across the media in some form or another: "It's all about you," "You deserve it," "Be independent," "Have your cake and eat it too!"

What a powerful way to deliver the Trojan horse! The English saying, "bread and circus," indicates a power's efforts to keep people fed and distracted in order to execute an agenda. The temple is the agenda, and we are no doubt now amusing ourselves to death while re-enforcing a very self-centered worldview on the way to the grave. Let's remember: "he sets himself up in the temple of God proclaiming to be God" (2 Thessalonians 2:4).

On the contrary, when we talk about being led by the Holy Spirit, we talk about being led by His inspiration. The word "amuse" has two parts "a," which means "to not," and "muse," which in a word means "inspiration." Interpretation: Unwittingly, we are building one huge wall with the enemy perched on the top. Our temples, therefore, have a massive internal defense system against walking by the Spirit.

We have established our premise that the Kingdom of God is accelerating into its fullness, and thus we should anticipate the kingdom of darkness doing the same. As we've established, there have never been more tools to captivate and transform the human soul than right now. Both kingdoms will aim to take full advantage.

A few years ago, IBM announced their predictions for computing's future, stating that within five years, all five senses will be involved. In their own words: *Touch: You will be able to touch through your phone, Sight: A pixel will be worth a thousand words, Hearing: Computers will hear what matters, Taste: Digital taste buds will help you to eat smarter, Smell: Computers will have a sense of smell.*

With more and more of our human senses being involved, our decisions about our own participation and involvement are more critical than ever, as we run the risk of being swept away into the world's current without realizing it. No doubt, the enemy's plans are to mitigate Christianity to a mere cultural or mental ascent, while we are unwitting to the fact of his ownership of our very soul. Thankfully, with God, all things are possible.

STARTING WITH SURRENDER

"Do not conform to the pattern of this world, but be transformed by the renewing of your mind. Then you will be able to test and approve what God's will is, his good, pleasing and perfect will." (Romans 12:2)

Thank God there is a solution! In fact, there is only one solution: we need to be completely renewed by His Holy Spirit within us. One big drag, especially for American Christians, is that renewal takes time, effort and intentionality. I believe that's why Paul preceded Romans 12:2 with Romans 12:1, "Therefore I urge you, brothers, on account of God's mercy, to offer your bodies as living sacrifices, holy and pleasing to God, which is your spiritual service of worship."

The temple was a place for sacrifices. Just because our microwave culture has lost track of that does not make it not true. Our body is to be a living sacrifice.

What does sacrifice look like? One way to look at sacrifice is killing something to please a god; another is to surrender something. We can beat our bodies into submission without netting a result. However, we can ponder the depths of the true cost of discipleship and recognize the foundation is surrender. When I first accepted Jesus as a child, the man asked something along the lines of "Are you ready to make Jesus the Lord of your life?"

I believe our generation has lost the context of what a Lord is. The definition of Lord is "someone or something having power, authority, or influence; a master or ruler." I believe the term "master" captures it best. We come under His authority and He becomes our master.

In scripture, we find we are also called friends, sons, kings and priests and even His brother, but He is first and always a good master. Considering the concept of master, do you believe a slave would simply do as he pleases? Or what he thought was a "good idea?" Naturally, the answer to both is no. A slave would only act in accordance with his orders.

After a period of training and instruction, the slave will learn how to please his master and anticipate his desires. Such is the same with Lordship. This brings us back to the concept of surrender. Paul's words "I no longer live…" come to mind. However, surrendering our will or self-determination is made difficult by the Trojan horse that has been strategically planted.

THE COST OF DISCIPLESHIP

In 1937 German Theologian Dietrich Bonhoeffer published his book titled The Cost of Discipleship. Bonhoeffer goes to great lengths to make the distinction between "cheap" and "costly" grace. In the book he states that "cheap grace is the preaching of forgiveness without requiring repentance, baptism without church discipline. Communion without confession. Cheap grace is grace without discipleship, grace without the cross, grace without Jesus Christ."

Cheap grace, Bonhoeffer says, is to hear the gospel preached as follows: "Of course you have sinned, but now everything is forgiven, so you can stay as you are and enjoy the consolations of forgiveness." In contrast "costly grace confronts us as a gracious call to follow Jesus, it comes as a word of forgiveness to the broken spirit and the contrite heart. It is costly because it compels a man to submit to the yoke of Christ and follow him; it is grace because Jesus says: 'My yoke is easy and my burden is light.'"

Bonhoeffer argues that as Christianity spread, the Church became "secularised", allowing genuine discipleship to the obedience of Jesus to give way to an "easier" form of Christian life. In this way, "the world was Christianised, and grace became its common property." But the hazard of this was that the gospel was cheapened, and obedience to the living Christ was gradually lost beneath formula and ritual, so that in the end, grace could literally be sold for monetary gain.

Awareness of the cost of discipleship is absolutely key here. Without full surrender, we are limited. Without awareness that "no good thing lives in me" (Romans 7:18), we will not surrender. If we still look at the things of this world as innocuous after we have come to Christ, what results is a verbal confession of faith, church attendance, and a growing visibility of "walking the Christian life?" How dangerous this is! Such leads only to "having a form of godliness and lacking the power thereof" (2 Timothy 3:5).

James says a doubleminded man is unstable in *all* his ways, not some. In America, we have embraced many "winds of doctrine" being presented in the name of the Lord. We have welcomed the mixture and called it diversity. We avoid scriptures pertaining to holiness and swing from demonic doctrines of religion without grace to demonic doctrines of grace that soft-soap the destructive nature of sin.

Can we get serious about the transformation process entails? By taking an objective look here, we have each had 20, 30, 40+ years or more embracing the devil's messaging, but we expect transformation at salvation? How foolish! Rather, if we have spent so many years in the world, how much more will we need to fill our eye and ear gates with His Voice, worship and His Word to transform our minds?

Do I offend you by suggesting we may need more than 15 minutes a day with the Lord to renew our thinking? Yet, that is what is often pawned as Christian prescription. Some is better than none, but what results should we expect? What result do you think 15 minutes in the morning and two hours of sitcoms at night will net? I dare suggest it may not be progress in your walk with Jesus.

Thank God that with Christ all things are possible! Let us not rely on the miraculous when we don't need a miracle, however. We simply need surrender and commitment. Both are a natural response to love, and "we love because He first loved us" (1 John 4:19). We love because He has washed us, made us clean, whole and right with Him.

As you read His Word through this sanctified lens, I promise your hunger for it will not only increase, but your old desires will fade away. As we commit to such a process, our bent toward religion and duty will want to appear. We will need a formula to remain free from trying to "earn" our way to Him.

THE WORK OF THE SPIRIT

"But if you bite and devour one another, take care that you are not consumed by one another. But I say, walk by the Spirit, and you will not carry out the desire of the flesh. For the flesh sets its desire against the Spirit, and the Spirit against the flesh; for these are in opposition to one another, so that you may not do the things that you please." (Galatians 5:15-17)

The Spirit is a consuming fire, sent to purify our temples so God can reside in a holy environment, ready for good works.

"I baptize you with water...He will baptize you with the Holy Spirit and fire." (Luke 3:16)

We are not alone in this endeavor. If the Spirit dwells within us, walking by the Spirit is our key to change. The fire of the Spirit is to consume its adversaries, to destroy all that stands in its way. The Holy Spirit is zealous to make us a holy temple. In order for this process to proceed, we must listen and yield to the same Spirit.

I've heard about yielding to the Spirit, but I often wondered what that practically looked like. I heard all the formulas and prescriptions, but I always wanted to understand what minute-to-minute Christian living was to look like. It can seem abstract without an example to see and follow. Trying our best, let's run through a hypothetical situation.

Let's say you are barely making your bills each month, you stop at a gas station while running late for work, and someone opens your passenger door and steals your cell phone while you're pumping gas. Based on your background and experiences, there are a myriad of reactions you can have in a moment like this. Fear, panic, rage, etc. You could run in and call the police, try to chase the perpetrator down in your car, sit down and cry, start drinking—on and on we go. As a growing Christian, you opt against one of the "worse" reactions and choose fear. You sit in your car and worry your butt off about not being able to afford another phone, losing your job, boyfriend, car, and as worry goes, things get out of hand and escalate.

You make it to work and your friend from church reminds you that Jesus said not to worry, so you decide to try. As you do, you end up focusing on your circumstances even more and things only get worse! You have spent so many years of your life handling problems this way, that incorporating Jesus' teachings are great in theory, but not of much practical value in the moment.

Does this process sound familiar? Perhaps it's the betrayal of a friend, loss of a job, financial/relational strain—the list goes on and on of our daily challenges on this earth. The question is: are we living by principles (religion and tree of knowledge of good and evil) or are we allowing His Spirit to transform us in each of these situations?

The renewal work we have done in the Word will help us immensely when we encounter daily troubles, because we will have the Word welling up inside when trouble arises. Even so, we need a default process of tuning in to the Spirit within during these moments (and all the non-crisis moments throughout our day), to start walking in the Spirit regularly. Good news! This is exactly the type of practical, supernatural Christian living we will be diving into in future chapters! It is a beautiful facet of Kingdom living.

Applying the basic principle of asking Jesus what He thinks in one of these situations, I avoided a "landmine" just a few days ago. My wife Rebekah is very gifted. One of her strongest gifts is in the area of hospitality, which also includes making the house look great! This is a wonderful gift that I benefit from often. That stated, since I am analytical, I can often get very inquisitive trying to "understand" certain purchases. I am sure your reaction to reading this is predictable based on your respective role in said dispute in your household!

We handle it much better now, but I will admit that this one has played out a bit over our 10 years of marriage. Just the other day, those old "questions" started rising up again. Rather than hammer her with them, I chose to ask the Lord what He thought. As I did, I tuned to vision and simply saw Him laughing. It may sound strange, but this was very disarming! From that picture, I gathered a) it was not a big deal, b) we are not headed for financial calamity, and c) I was probably safe to drop it without saying anything.

I consider this one example of practically walking by the Spirit in an everyday situation. I did not gratify the desires of the flesh (the demand for an explanation that I could understand), and rather was more interested in Jesus' thoughts on the matter.

PRAYER IN THE TEMPLE

This brings us back to us being temples of the Holy Spirit. Our God's desire is to "tabernacle" with us. To dwell inside so we can enjoy intimate fellowship. Somehow this was lost on me as a child. "Inviting Jesus into my heart" sounded good, but lacked context. The verbiage was spot on, though, because that's right where we want Him and right where He wanted to be! Growing up in church, the saying was so familiar, its depth of meaning was lost. Praying to a far-away invisible God was the picture, but "Jesus living inside my heart" were the words.

I have since learned I'm praying to a God that resides in me! So praying is more like talking to myself, or rather Him inside! In return, I receive profoundly amazing and peace-giving answers to my questions!

Am I the first? I was relieved to learn when Elohim (plural of God) said "let's make man in our image" in Genesis 1, He was talking to Himself. Deuteronomy 6:4 states, "Hear, O Israel: The Lord our God, the Lord is one." The Lord is one. And so are we to be with Him. The Lord wants to be one with us. This is temple. Full relationship with constant access. Just like your arms and legs with your mind. Each movement of a limb has an origination in the mind, but they are so organically connected that actions are seamless. The imagery of God being far away needs to be wiped out and replaced. Our God dwells seamlessly.

As a brief summary, we are vessels intended to be filled with God's Spirit and presence. Even after receiving His Spirit there is still work to be done. He can only work in us to the extent we surrender to Him and allow Him to work.

As newborn babes, we must learn how to walk spiritually. If we do not, we will operate from a worldview (the Trojan horse) that has been firmly entrenched by the kingdom of darkness. Even as we learn to walk, we must be careful not to slip into religion, which creates bondage. However, we can take confidence that "where the Spirit of the Lord is there is freedom" (2 Corinthians 3:17).

There are two ways to keep the Law, which is good, and here to protect us. One is to seek to try to do it by ourselves. The other is to walk by the Spirit. God's abiding presence in our vessels enables us to and walk by the Spirit. His presence is the only thing that allows us to live the supernatural lives we were made to live.

WORSHIP

We have covered a lot of ground thus far. We have looked into God's plan and His long view of history, unearthed mysteries in the Law, openly wondered about the apparent languishing of the church, and then we got practical. There is yet another aspect of the eternal Kingdom we must understand before exploring what we consider to be the supernatural elements. That aspect is worship.

There is an old joke about cats and dogs view of the world. A dog says, "You pet me, you feed me, you shelter me, you love me. You must be God." A cat says the same exact thing but comes to a different conclusion: "You pet me, you feed me, you shelter me, you love me. I must be God."

The Bible is a book about God and His Kingdom, but recent generations of western Christianity have turned it into a book about us. We go to it for solutions, for help, for guidance and it does provide all of those things, but we are not the point. He is.

Our view of the world as cats creates a grid to where our teaching, our learning, our daily activities are all generally centered on us. This "consumerism" is certainly reinforced in all media, advertising and every outlet of the kingdom of this world, but most concerning is how it has filtered into the Christian world. This approach to Christ and His Kingdom will only leave us empty, "for in Him we live and move and have our being" (Acts 17:28).

Since our preconceptions, formed by our grid, guide what we see, we simply need a different grid. In other words, if we think the Bible is about us or if we think God just wants us to "behave," then guess what we will see when we read His Word? Pitifully, everything we read will only strengthen our position, because what we have predetermined will be confirmed with every word.

On the other hand, if we indeed believe God is making us to be like Him, then everything we encounter will confirm this powerful Truth. Since our natural eyes and understanding have been perverted by this world, this Truth will require a Spiritual re-interpretation of all we see (walking by the Spirit).

"He has made us competent as ministers of a new covenant--not of the letter but of the Spirit; for the letter kills, but the Spirit gives life." (2 Corinthians 3:6)

Our distorted lens has been entrenched by our western thinking and consumer based approach Christianity. It needs to be redeemed by the Spirit. Without it, sermon after sermon, study after study, we will be killed by the exact letter we've embraced. So we must press into what brings the abundant life. Life in the Spirit.

Let's go on a treasure hunt in His Word to explore where our life is actually found. He knows what we need, and as we seek and praise Him, He will pour out His Spirit on us by meeting our deepest needs. By worshipping Him we will find:

- Health and Blessing: **"Worship the LORD your God, and his blessing will be on your food and water. I will take away sickness from among you."** (Exodus 23:25)

- True Comfort: **"Praise be to the God and Father of our Lord Jesus Christ, the Father of compassion and the God of all comfort."** (2 Corinthians 1:3)

- Expansion of the Kingdom: **"They broke bread in their homes and ate together with glad and sincere hearts, praising God and enjoying the favor of all the people. And the Lord added to their number daily those who were being saved."** (Acts 2:46)

- Real Perspective: **"At this, Job got up and tore his robe and shaved his head. Then he fell to the ground in worship and said: "Naked I came from my mother's womb, and naked I will depart. The Lord gave and the Lord has taken away; may the name of the Lord be praised."** (Job 1:20-21)

- Answers to Questions: **"While they were worshiping the Lord and fasting, the Holy Spirit said, 'Set apart for me Barnabas and Saul for the work to which I have called them.'"** (Acts 13:2)

This list could go on and on. The reality is that as we praise and worship, God's provision comes into daily struggles and challenges. He created us to worship, and as we do, He pours heavenly provision right back on us.

Worship is the culture of heaven, so as we worship we can manifest heaven and participate in His prayer so His will can be done on earth as it is in heaven. His will is for His Kingdom to be established throughout the earth. In His Kingdom there is no longer sickness, despair, grief, pain, fear or any other thing that brings hardship to our lives.

THE EXTREME LIFESTYLE OF WORSHIP

Worship is a lifestyle of focusing on Him. It is a byproduct of everything we do in this world as we walk in the Spirit and invite Him into our jobs, families, activities, and everything we do throughout the day. As we do, we experience His joy and provision for our lives. He lifts us up, and as He does, song becomes a very natural spontaneous reaction. Paul even said we can teach, admonish, and get all wisdom through the songs the Spirit gives us!

"Let the message of Christ dwell among you richly as you teach and admonish one another with all wisdom through psalms, hymns, and songs from the Spirit, singing to God with gratitude in your hearts." (Colossians 3:16)

How seriously did Paul take worship?

The crowd joined in the attack against Paul and Silas, and the magistrates ordered them to be stripped and beaten with rods. After they had been severely flogged, they were thrown into prison, and the jailer was commanded to guard them carefully. When he received these orders, he put them in the inner cell and fastened their feet in the stocks.

"About midnight Paul and Silas were praying and singing hymns to God, and the other prisoners were listening to them. Suddenly there was such a violent earthquake that the foundations of the prison were shaken. At once all the prison doors flew open, and everyone's chains came loose. The jailer woke up, and when he saw the prison doors open, he drew his sword and was about to kill himself because he thought the prisoners had escaped. But Paul shouted, 'Don't harm yourself! We are all here!'

"The jailer called for lights, rushed in and fell trembling before Paul and Silas. He then brought them out and asked, 'Sirs, what must I do to be saved?'

"They replied, 'Believe in the Lord Jesus, and you will be saved—you and your household.' Then they spoke the word of the Lord to him and to all the others in his house. At that hour of the night the jailer took them and washed their wounds; then immediately he and all his household were baptized. The jailer brought them into his house and set a meal before them; he was filled with joy because he had come to believe in God— he and his whole household." (Acts 16:22-34)

This is extreme. Paul and Silas were so convinced about the power of worship they did it while bloodied, beaten, and imprisoned with chains. Their worship caused a reaction in the heavenly realm so strong that it caused an earthquake to open the doors and break off their chains! Their freedom then led to the jailer's freedom. Do you know we often need our own chains removed before we can set others free? As you become a worshipper, you will be able to watch them fall off.

UNCONDITIONAL WORSHIP

Just as our tendency is toward conditional love, our tendency is toward conditional worship. When you are walking in the Spirit, that changes. Even if you are not "feeling spiritual" and the chips are down, if you have made a commitment to a lifestyle of worship you just do it, knowing God's goodness and provision is coming.

"Although the fig tree shall not blossom, neither shall fruit be in the vines; the labor of the olive shall fail, and the fields shall yield no meat; the flock shall be cut off from the fold, and there shall be no herd in the stalls Yet I will rejoice in the LORD, I will joy in the God of my salvation." (Habakkuk 3:17-18)

Has my worship of God been conditional or unconditional?

You may think, "that's just not practical, I can't just spend my whole life worshipping. How am I going to pay my bills?" Don't we need to focus on our own provision? I mean, that's literally what we've been trained to do since we've entered this world! Well, in a word, you don't have to worry.

"And why do you worry about clothes? See how the flowers of the field grow. They do not labor or spin. Yet I tell you that not even Solomon in all his splendor was dressed like one of these. If that is how God clothes the grass of the field, which is here today and tomorrow is thrown into the fire, will he not much more clothe you—you of little faith? So do not worry, saying, 'What shall we eat?' or 'What shall we drink?' or 'What shall we wear?' For the pagans run after all these things, and your heavenly Father knows that you need them. But seek first his kingdom and his righteousness, and all these things will be given to you as well." (Matthew 6:28-33)

Worship is seeking first His Kingdom. As you learn to focus on Jesus and tune into the flow of His Spirit throughout the day, worship will flow as well. You will find that the Spirit of Jesus, which is also the Spirit of Knowledge, will provide answers for those daily challenges that have been sidelining you.

Where the Spirit of the Lord is, there is freedom! Freedom from your struggles with your circumstances, freedom from your habits, freedom from yourself! As the saying goes, wherever you go, there you are. Usually the problem is us! So as we learn to focus on Jesus throughout our days, we learn the heart of worship and become worshippers.

"My mouth is filled with your praise, declaring your splendor all day long." (Psalms 71:8)

"Let everything that has breath praise the Lord. Praise the Lord." (Psalms 150:6)

As you may have noticed, the term "surrender" has come up a lot. The reality is that the Lord can only work with what we give Him. Worship is one of the most powerful signs of surrender there is. It's foolishness in the natural, as nothing seems to be getting accomplished, but the victory is in surrender. It shows a level of trust and hope in God that magnifies His presence and summons the angelic. It's no wonder Satan hates it when we worship God.

When the chips are down, he expects us to turn on each other like we usually do. He loves to camp out in our weakest moments. Just like he came to Jesus at the end of the 40 days of temptation in the wilderness, his goal is to come to you in your most vulnerable moment. Without realizing it, we often entertain and agree with our adversary's voice in these times rather than turning to thankfulness.

"Finally, be strong in the Lord and in his mighty power. Put on the full armor of God, so that you can take your stand against the devil's schemes. For our struggle is not against flesh and blood, but against the rulers, against the authorities, against the powers of this dark world and against the spiritual forces of evil in the heavenly realms. Therefore, put on the full armor of God, so that when the day of evil comes, you may be able to stand your ground, and after you have done

everything, to stand. Stand firm then, with the belt of truth buckled around your waist, with the breastplate of righteousness in place, and with your feet fitted with the readiness that comes from the gospel of peace. In addition to all this, take up the shield of faith, with which you can extinguish all the flaming arrows of the evil one. Take the helmet of salvation and the sword of the Spirit, which is the word of God." (Ephesians 6:10-17)

WORSHIPPING TO ADVANCE

The Kingdom life is about advancing. When there is an enemy attack, we do not retreat, we stand. We do not lose ground, we stand and trust our equipment. Too often we lose ground during these attacks. Rather than standing on the truth and turning to worship, we agree with the voice of compromise and division and become conflicted. In these defining moments, we often make our biggest life mistakes. We lose perspective and miss the realization that a few minutes of worship can yield a dramatically different result. Thankfully, we are no longer unaware!

"But we do not belong to those who shrink back and are destroyed, but to those who have faith and are saved." (Hebrews 10:39)

When situations look bleakest, when our thoughts are unclear and all seems in disarray, we worship. Allowing these very same trials to develop perseverance brings us to maturity rather than ruin. The key is making it through the trial without compromise. Worship opens the door.

Worship changes the atmosphere, because it is simple active resistance. James tells us if we resist the devil he will flee from us. Worshiping God in a moment of difficulty can be your go-to tactic of resistance. It sends a bold statement that every time something difficult comes your way, you are going to "go with what you know." What you know is that God is still on the throne. He loves

111

you and He is going to inhabit your praise. As you do that, the grip is quickly broken and your perspective on the trial will become a heavenly one.

WORSHIP AS A RESPONSE TO AN INNER REALITY

Worship is supernatural. Something about praising God invites angels and a heavenly presence. We learn in the Word that worship is a big part of heaven's culture. Despite centuries of misleading and inaccurate depictions of heaven, we will not be sitting on a cloud playing a harp all the time. However, it is clear that our natural reaction to His presence is worship. Heaven is all about His presence, and His presence brings peace and inner completion.

Even on earth, what happens when people have inner excitement? How do you know when someone is in love? Do they not seem to walk around in constant song? Somehow, song is a very spontaneous reaction to inner joy and excitement. Genuine worship is the same. We don't worship because we have to or because that is the culture, we worship because of what is happening inside of us.

As we walk in the spirit and enjoy his friendship and counsel in our innermost being, everything we do turns into worship. The work we do with our hands, the relationships we have, even our hobbies become expressions of worship. Our inner joy needs an outlet in that outlet is spontaneous, creative and uplifting.

"But in your hearts revere Christ as Lord. Always be prepared to give an answer to everyone who asks you to give the reason for the hope that you have..." (1 Peter 3:15)

The statistics show an overwhelming majority of Christians have never shared their faith. Perhaps it is because people are not asking? When you live life as a worshipper, people will be asking. People will ask because your hope is evident. Our lives are a form of worship. Rather than simply living for ourselves or the selfish pursuits of this world, a worshipper's life is evidence of someone living for more. Since that is what we were all made for, people will want what you have.

In fact, I have to even be careful when speaking about a worshipper's life. All of us are worshippers, but not all of our objects of worship bring life. There is only One who brings life. So all of us are worshippers, either idol worshippers or worshippers of God. If you don't currently consider yourself a worshipper of God, perhaps you should take a moment to consider if this is true.

Do I agree that God created me to be a worshipper? If I am not currently a worshipper of God, where has my worship been directed?

As you walk and praise in the Spirit, you will receive His counsel and He will lead you into all truth. You have no need for anyone to teach you.

"As for you, the anointing you received from him remains in you, and you do not need anyone to teach you. But as his anointing teaches you about all things and as that anointing is real, not counterfeit—just as it has taught you, remain in him." (1 John 2:27)

The Spirit will lead you to worship. The Holy Spirit is the Spirit of worship and the Spirit of truth. As we learn to lean into a lifestyle of praise and worship, He will purge the false things out of our hearts.

"God is Spirit, and his worshipers must worship in the Spirit and in truth." (John 4:24)

God loves honesty. Genuine worship is a spiritual act but it is also a truthful act. He is King! We are not. We can go through the motions of something that is called worship, or we can actually worship. Actual worship is bowing down. Actual worship has always been depicted as people on the ground before the one being worshiped. This seems quite evil when a man is desiring this type of adoration, but it is the opposite with the One who deserves it.

ALLOWING HIM TO LIFT US UP AS WE WORSHIP

He knows how he made us and he says this is good for us. Somehow, in worshiping Him, the cravings for the other things we may be inclined to worship lose their grip on our souls.

When we worship in Truth, we are remembering that we are dust and He fearfully and wonderfully gathered that dust together and breathed life into it. This perspective shifts our views from the weeds down in the dust, to the trees as we rise with Him, to the forest, and then to the eagle's, as He gives us His view. His view gives us expectancy for breakthrough. Even corporately pouring our hearts out to the Lord raises our collective expectation of His goodness.

"And we know that in all things God works for the good of those who love him, who have been called according to his purpose." (Romans 8:28)

As we lay down all of our concerns at the altar and ask for Him to address them, we are set free. The truth is that we have a little control over the many circumstances that affect us on a daily basis. As we worship, we are able to express the casting of our cares onto the one who cares for us, expecting goodness in return.

If there be anything that blocks you from worshiping earnestly, it will be revealed. As you recognize your very basic rules of worship, and struggle to worship, ask Him. He will show you the idols or blockages that are preventing you from bowing to Him. If we cannot bow to Him and worship, but we agree His ways are good and true, we want these things dealt with. Worship has a way of bringing it all to the surface.

An environment of worship is the perfect backdrop for ministry and for meeting the needs of people. You get to feel His heart and get a stronger sense of what He wants to do. Doing what He wants to do brings breakthrough in people's lives, *human will accomplishes nothing (John 6:63).* We recognize this as critical as we begin to step out in the gifts of the Spirit.

Worship invites the presence of God. His presence brings His instruction and His power. The cloud of His presence is leading us out of the wilderness and entering the Promised Land, and we want to follow it. Let us learn what environment cultivates the hosting of His presence.

The book of Psalms is rich with praise of the Most High. Reading it can help turn you into a worshipper. The book ends with six beautiful chapters on praise and worship. Take time to read the final six chapters, allowing your heart to be fully present to each verse as you read. Turn your heart to Him and learn the art of praise. Walk out this path of praise into His Presence.

"Enter His gates with thanksgiving and His courts with praise; give thanks to him and praise His name." (Psalms 100:4)

CHAPTER 8:

A Joshua Family

I recently read the story of ten-year-old Tobias Bass. His long term plan is to be an Army pastor. With uncommon faith and foresight, young Tobias asked God to one day allow him to bring comfort to soldiers. Although Tobias was already keyed into his long term calling, what stood out about this story was the boy's faithfulness and heart.

Tobias' older brother Titus was born with cerebral palsy. Watching his brother spend his days watching other children play, Tobias set a goal to help him do exactly that. Determined to help his brother, he sent a letter to a local news station asking for help obtaining a jogging stroller. His goal was to push his brother successfully through a 5K.

In his letter the boy wrote "my mom is a teacher and can't afford one of those fancy running pushing joggers and all I have to use is a baby pushing stroller". Can you go on the news and not ask Oklahomans to give me anything but can someone loan me a jogger pusher so I can push Titus in the 5K?"

The TV station helped orchestrate the gift of a jogging stroller for Tobias and Titus and the boys successfully accomplished their feat. After doing so, Tobias has run other races and even successfully pushed other handicapped children through them.

When it comes to loving a child of God, nothing is mundane. Whether we help someone with their dream or simply speak words of life over another, it matters. More than the individual achievements and tasks we accomplish, the people we love are the precious things that remain in the heavenly registry. When we are serving God, we naturally serve those made in His image.

"But if serving the LORD seems undesirable to you, then choose for yourselves this day whom you will serve, whether the gods your ancestors served beyond the Euphrates, or the gods of the Amorites, in whose land you are living. But as for me and my household, we will serve the LORD." (Joshua 24:15)

From the beginning of time, God has chosen to work through the structure of family. He tells His story and teaches us His ways through the simplicity of the things in front of us. He challenges us by entrusting people into our care, and wants to guide us to enter into the peace, provision, and rest of His Kingdom along with the other people He has given to us.

There is, however, a challenge with loving the people right in front of us. They're right in front of us all the time! The entire situation of loving people comes to a head. This chapter is about our families. If you do not have children yet, take this as a time to learn now. Everything discussed also applies to other family members and friends, as God has seen fit to put them into your life for a reason.

FAMILY AS A PLACE OF PERFECTING

Families are a place of perfecting. Our God is a practical God and He has chosen to work through family as a small and practical kingdom. This detail is not lost on the adversary. God uses what's in front of us to teach and train us, while Satan wants to use the same to destroy us.

Since we know God is focused on training us to rule and reign with Him as a family forever, we come to learn how important this training really is. How do we love and unite with the ones God has strategically predetermined to be in our earthly families?

117

Let me re-emphasize: in His sovereignty, God has strategically predetermined every member of our friends and families. Could these critical details possibly be lost on a good Father?

The spouse we wake up to every day, the children who will depend on us for a few decades (or a lifetime, in some cases), the parents we are to honor, the siblings we grow up with, and the friends, co-workers, neighbors, and classmates are all strategically selected. If His goal is to train us to conquer, would He waste these details? Would He rather encircle us with amiable, well-behaved, awesome people who are in no need of training themselves?

There is no doubt that family is often the source of our greatest grief in this life, but also our greatest joy, peace and acceptance. It is usually the place where we learn our most profound lessons, so it is a favorite teaching tool of our King. As a place of perfecting, it is usually the place where we are faced with the reality of our natural tendency towards very conditional love. "You do this and *then* I will…" We do this with spouses, as we parent, and as we are raised. Do something wrong and you usually get a scowl, punishment, a negative tone of voice or all three!

We control and manipulate family members all day long with our subtle glances, voice inflections, and background intel on one another, through any means necessary to get our desired outcome. Many of our views on love have been formed by the world through media. As covered in the last chapter, this messaging makes us very selfish. Our spouses are supposed to treat us the way we want, because we're supposed to get what we want, right?

A SEEMINGLY IMPOSSIBLE STANDARD

With our own conditional love and the conditional love of others smack dab in our face daily, we are faced with a terrific growing opportunity in light of the Gospel. As we grow in Christ and His love leads, undoubtedly, family can become the place where we will first experience God's Heavenly Kingdom on the earth. As with His all-encompassing Kingdom, everything starts at the top, though. Let's look at a dynamic that is only made possible by the Spirit of God.

"Wives, submit yourselves to your own husbands as you do to the Lord. For the husband is the head of the wife as Christ is the head of the church, his body, of which he is the Savior. Now as the church submits to Christ, so also wives should submit to their husbands in everything. Husbands, love your wives, just as Christ loved the church and gave himself up for her to make her holy, cleansing her by the washing with water through the word, and to present her to himself as a radiant church, without stain or wrinkle or any other blemish, but holy and blameless. In this same way, husbands ought to love their wives as their own bodies. He who loves his wife loves himself. After all, no one ever hated their own body, but they feed and care for their body, just as Christ does the church for we are members of his body. 'For this reason a man will leave his father and mother and be united to his wife, and the two will become one flesh.' This is a profound mystery, but I am talking about Christ and the church. However, each one of you also must love his wife as he loves himself, and the wife must respect her husband." (Ephesians 5:22-33)

Is there a more debated (and avoided) passage in our modern context? Jesus tells His listeners they must eat His flesh and that offends the people of His time, but this one is multiple times more offensive in our current world. How did we get so off course? Perhaps the Holy Spirit's plan would have never required the women's liberation movement?

The desire of a woman's true heart is to be loved and cherished the way Jesus loves and cherishes His own body. This is not only possible, but it is His design and intention for us to discover this mystery. That stated, it is impossible for a husband to do this for any length of time without full surrender to Jesus and His Spirit's ways. A husband must first receive love from His Father and learn how to walk in His Spirit's ways before he can love well.

SUBMISSION TO AUTHORITY

We must remember God's plans are good; they bring real joy, peace, and real love. Indeed, if we are to experience the Kingdom in our homes it must first be an internal reality for the husband so he can love as Christ loves. This fits right into God's training for reigning plans for us. Let's look at a wife's role (and how it is equally rigged!)

"When Jesus had finished saying all this to the people who were listening, he entered Capernaum. There a centurion's servant, whom his master valued highly, was sick and about to die. The centurion heard of Jesus and sent some elders of the Jews to him, asking him to come and heal his servant…He was not far from the house when the centurion sent friends to say to him: 'Lord, don't trouble yourself, for I do not deserve to have you come under my roof…But say the word, and my servant will be healed. <u>For I myself am a man under authority</u>, with soldiers under me. I tell this one, "Go," and he goes; and that one, "Come," and he comes. I say to my servant, "Do this," and he does it.' <u>When Jesus heard this, he was amazed</u> at him, and turning to the crowd following him, he said, 'I tell you, I have not found such great faith even in Israel.' Then the men who had been sent returned to the house and found the servant well." (Luke 7:1-10)

You may be wondering what this passage has to do with marriage. The Roman centurion's understanding of authority amazed Jesus. It is the only time in the gospels we see Jesus having this type of response to someone's understanding of how the Kingdom works.

The passage in Ephesians requires us to have a similar understanding of Kingdom to comprehend it. Like the centurion, both husbands and wives are under authority. Our lives in Christ simply do not work unless we trust Him enough to surrender and submit our lives to His amazing and trustworthy authority.

Thousands of pages could be written on this topic alone, but let's believe the Word and leave it at this: In Christ, men can love their wives and truly be that amazing and trustworthy authority that wives, in Christ, can submit to. In fulfilling the Spirit's call to unity here, we get a picture of what God's Kingdom looks like and can allow heaven to manifest in our homes.

WITNESSING A MIRACLE

"For we are God's handiwork, created in Christ Jesus to do good works, which God prepared in advance for us to do." (Ephesians 2:10)

There is another beautiful aspect of God on display in family. We get to experience, close up, a song that God is writing. The word Paul uses here is *poiema*, from which we get the English word poem. Being in someone's life is to see God's story unfold in another. If you allow the Spirit to transform your lens (how you view the world), you can get an up-close look at a masterpiece being made—right at home in each of your family members! Doesn't feel like that sometimes? It is time to ask God for His words for that person.

He loves every one of us and has even numbered the hairs on our heads (Luke 12:7). We can get a constant, fresh revelation of unconditional love for a person as we filter our thoughts with the Spirit's words for them.

"How precious also are Your thoughts to me, O God! How vast is the sum of them! Were I to count them, they would outnumber the grains of sand..." (Psalms 139:17-18)

If His thoughts for us are that numerous, then logically, we can tune into those thoughts for a person at any time. Whether it's a suggestion to push your brother through a 5k like Tobias or simply a prompt to call someone, He is speaking and He wants us to listen to learn His heart. When someone seems unlovable and we hear His heart for that person, what will that do for our own heart when we feel unlovable?

121

Family is indeed what He has put right in front of us to learn His ways. As we tune to Him, we learn about the Kingdom. If we approach family as the classroom and the Holy Spirit as the teacher, we will learn. We each display God's glory uniquely, and as we grow in Him, His manifold glory will be on display in our homes (Ephesians 3:10.)

Have you been able to recognize God's handiwork in those around you?

PARENTING WITH GOD

This is not a lesson on how to fix your family problems. Rather, it is an encouragement to trust and learn to listen to a bigger God. To hear the words of His heart and partner with Him. This is both essential and practical in our role as parents.

"Children, obey your parents in the Lord, for this is right. 'Honor your father and mother'—which is the first commandment with a promise— 'so that it may go well with you and that you may enjoy long life on the earth.' Fathers, do not exasperate your children; instead, bring them up in the training and instruction of the Lord." (Ephesians 6:1-4)

Continuing with the theme of authority and God's Kingdom, we see the Fifth Commandment. This is the very first commandment for our dealings with one another (the first four were between us and God). As parents, do we enforce this in our homes? Authority structures are not very clear in our modern culture. Most media outlets portray children running the show to a small—or even great—extent. It is a subtle, but insidious attack on the very foundation of the Kingdom (the authority of Jesus Christ).

Children are to submit to a good authority that loves and cares for them. If they do not, society will crumble. That is why this is the first commandment with a promise. **Children honor...so you will live long in the land** (Exodus 20:12). Everything is undermined if the most basic unit doesn't function as God designed it to, because submission to a good authority is the way of the Kingdom. If children do not learn this in their homes, their own foundations will not be put in place.

Children need to experience what we need to experience. Good authority, as demonstrated by the tender love and firm discipline administered by a loving authority.

DISCIPLINE

"And have you completely forgotten this word of encouragement that addresses you as a father addresses his son? It says, 'My son, do not make light of the Lord's discipline, and do not lose heart when he rebukes you, because the Lord disciplines the one he loves, and he chastens everyone he accepts as his son.'" (Hebrews 12:5-6)

All God's children are under authority. Since family is a microcosm of Kingdom, parents have added context for understanding God's ways. We understand the importance of discipline for our children, and this can be reluctantly applied to God's role with us. If our earthly orientation has been great parenting, we probably experienced the productivity of good discipline.

On the other hand, for the many who did not, submission to God's authority and even discipline is difficult. Abuse of authority elicits a protective response. We must consider if a negative earthly experience with authority has caused us to protect ourselves from God's loving authority and discipline.

How would this look? Well, how does a lack of trust in a relationship look to you? We control, compartmentalize, and withhold. "God, you can have my Sunday morning, but at work I have to focus on work." "God, you can have my 10%, but I'm going to worry and stress about all 100%." "God, you can have my heart, but I'm going to occupy my mind with the cares of this world."

We can unknowingly do this with God, and it can greatly limit the work He can do in our lives. If you are a parent, think about your children. How would your parenting be affected if your child didn't trust you? What would be the effectiveness of your approaches to discipline if your child withheld, compartmentalized, and controlled your relationship?

We gain a glimpse of God's protective heart when we view His discipline through the lens of love. His desire is to protect us from evil. Jesus came to destroy the works of Satan (1 John 3:8), so if we submit to His authority and discipline, you can be sure His work will be to destroy Satan's work in your life.

A BATTLE FOR OUR CHILDREN

We can agree that God's desire is to protect us, because that is our desire for our children. There is a battle going on for their hearts and minds. We must be proactive, for our part, because we know the enemy will not be complacent with his. This concept was not original in its time, but let's explore the enemy's plans for our children.

"He alone who owns the youth, gains the future... The state must declare the child to be the most precious treasure of the people. As long as the government is perceived as working for the benefit of the children, the people will happily endure almost any curtailment of liberty and almost any deprivation." (Adolf Hitler, Mein Kampf)

Shall we perceive the Third Reich of Hitler's time differently from how we perceive "the world?" Heaven forbid. At some points in history, the enemy's plans have been on full display for all to see, while at other times they have been less obvious. We must use the more obvious times to help us understand his strategy for the less obvious times. Here we learn he wants to train our kids, so we must be aware and diligent to train them ourselves! This requires wisdom from above.

PARENTING WITH THE SPIRIT OF WISDOM

If nothing else on this earth will drive you to surrender and be led by the Spirit, it is parenting another human being. The frustrations and internal emotional swings can leave our words unchecked. These very words can bring life or death in any given moment, so if you have gone about parenting in the flesh for a while, you can relate.

Let me just submit to you: this is rigged by God for our good. If we are reflective, it is also rigged so we will see His extreme grace. He has set us free and patiently loved us through our shortcomings. The rigging is so we learn the only way, the way of the Spirit. Words and reactions from the Spirit bring healing. Paul instructs us not to provoke our children to anger. Parenting without the Spirit has this exact effect!

"Start children off on the way they should go, and even when they are old they will not turn from it." (Proverbs 22:6)

What is the way they should go? The way of His Kingdom. As our Father, He chose grace to mediate our differences so we could be right with Him. We can do the same. It takes extreme grace to raise children well. After all, it is madness to believe our children will one day hear and obey God's voice if they haven't done it at home with us. Thankfully, with God, all things are possible. Nonetheless, we need patience, grace, and much wisdom to both well demonstrate and teach our children the precepts of authority.

We can learn from His ways to get the moment-by-moment wisdom we need. This comes from walking in the Spirit in our parenting. It is a learned practice. We must first see that we don't have the tools and recognize His rigging. We must see there is simply no other way to properly steward the lives of those little ones!

Why is this chapter on family so important as we attempt to come out of the wilderness? We will not be trusted with more until we have been faithful with what has been given to us already.

"Whoever can be trusted with very little can also be trusted with much, and whoever is dishonest with very little will also be dishonest with much." (Luke 16:10)

If we are not loving our wives, submitting to our husbands, or raising our children in the ways of the Lord, should we expect to be trusted with the souls of many? If we take the call to make disciples of all the earth seriously, and recognize it is our role and calling to advance His Kingdom, we must put first things first. The Kingdom must first be advanced in our own home.

THE KINGDOM AT HOME

Seeing the Kingdom advanced in our home provides us with a practical testimony that will be used to radically impact others. When you are able to share the miracles the Lord worked in your life through resurrecting broken relationships, the Kingdom advances. As you learn to submit your plans and battles to Him at home, the Kingdom advances. As your experience with Him grows, your faith increases. Others are then able to borrow from your faith when you share your family transformation story.

I write about the restoration of family after seeing the resurrection of my own. After starting off our marriage with six very difficult years, the Lord started the restoration process in our home after healing each of our hearts. Rebekah and I both brought hurts and habits into our marriage. Being around each other seemed to bring them all to the surface.

Coming from a broken home and suffering abandonment as a child, Rebekah was fiercely independent. My own reaction from past wounds was to appease and control people while manipulating outcomes (awful, I know!) So our eventual conflict was inevitable. Pain bordering on hopelessness ensued. We were "churched" and did the American "Christian life" well, but checking the right boxes never solved the deeper issues of the heart. Transformation was needed, but our culture led us to have a few drinks and sweep it all under the rug!

Had it not been for the wife-sized mirror in front of me, I could have fallen for the delusion of thinking all was fine. Doing well by every American "measurable," I could have even convinced myself that I loved well. However, the lack of change in the woman in front of me was impossible for an honest man to ignore. Loved people grow in love, and that wasn't happening. The fault was mine, but I didn't know how to fix what I only sensed broken.

We sought counsel from "healthy" Christian couples, but examples of what looked like success turned out to be illusions as we got closer. What were a healthy Christian marriage and home supposed to look like? No couples we knew set the bar at heaven, so we encountered lots of the alternative.

In His sovereignty and perfection of timing, the Lord brought healing to my heart in a number of stages. After one of the most profound weekends of healing, at a men's weekend, I announced to Rebekah that I was going to fight for her and fight for our marriage. She didn't share it at the time, but after Jesus brought healing and breakthrough to her own heart, she confessed the desire that awoke inside when she saw me after that men's weekend. She decided she wanted what I had, and described my countenance as "glowing."

Is that not how God intended Christianity to work? You can't give away what you don't possess. I tried for so long to point out what was wrong with her and what she needed to fix, but after something got fixed in *me*, everything changed. She opened her heart to Jesus and He brought her into a beautiful journey of trust and surrender.

INNER HEALING BEFORE RELATIONAL HEALING

There are places in our hearts that simply cannot be accessed until we have learned how to trust Him with others. The term "peeling back the onion" has probably been overused, but it is a good analogy. Perhaps the heart of flesh is encased in the heart of stone and some of those layers have to come off first, before He can get to the deepest areas?

As we allow ourselves to journey with Him back into painful memories, we can ask Him where He was at the time. Was He present in our suffering? As we tune into the Spirit, we can access and revisit those memories not alone, but with Him. In those places, accompanied by the I Am, our stories can get a proper re-interpretation. He is the editor. The story doesn't change, but how we see it changes dramatically.

We get to see and experience firsthand that He never abandoned us. If we felt alone, this moment can feel like a rewrite. Beautiful scars are formed where there was an open wound. Call it inner healing or whatever you desire, but going through this process allows Jesus to heal our deepest parts and change how we interact with the ones we love. Rather than living out of a place of reaction, we are enabled to interact from a loved and healed place. We are able to open ourselves up to His instruction during the moments that make up our day, instead of speaking or reacting from past wounds. We become teachable, saying "Lord, allow Your Kingdom to be formed within me so it can be formed around me."

It is appropriate God brought healing to our marriage in our seventh year. The first six years brought a lot of work in trying to fix each other, but in the seventh year the Lord brought us Sabbath. As we learned to rest more, instead of trying to fix and control one another, He increased our confidence in surrendering more battles to Him.

There is a process to everything in life. Perhaps some people surrender their lives to Jesus and pray about everything from that day forward, but others of us learn to trust and surrender over time. God has shown me enough that I can confidently push "all in" to His will and plan, but getting here has been a process.

I can't go back to my old way of living. It no longer works. I've seen and experienced enough with God to return to a place of ignorance. I previously lived out married life in the definition of insanity: I did the same things over and over again, yet expected a different result. Even if I learned all the right tactics, how could I love well with a heart of stone? I needed to first allow God to give me a heart of flesh. This happened through trust and surrender, which came as a result of experiencing His healing of my past.

I'm so thankful for the timing of the healing to our marriage. Rebekah and I were already four years down the road in re-producing our collective wounds from another life. Our oldest daughter's first four years were with two parents living out of places in our hearts that caused *us* to act like four-year-olds!

SYMMETRY IN OUR LIVES

If the Lord had not brought healing to our hearts, we could have carried massive regret later in life. We were on our way to constructing barriers in our daughter's heart. While checking all the observable Christian boxes, we missed the most essential ones.

"Woe to you, teachers of the law and Pharisees, you hypocrites! You give a tenth of your spices - mint, dill and cumin. But you have neglected the more important matters of the law - justice, mercy and faithfulness. You should have practiced the latter, without neglecting the former." (Matthew 23:23)

If we continued down our path, our hypocrisy would have been a massive obstacle for Sydney as she reconciled faith with her experiences. Thankfully, the Lord has shown us the beauty and importance of allowing Him to form His Kingdom in our home. He has helped us love each other in ways we never thought possible. Now, we experience moments and even days that would even seem unbelievable if I saw them on a sitcom (even ones from the 50s).

I am honored to share this with you. Our breakthrough is for your own. It is always okay to borrow from someone else's faith when you need it, and even from their story. Just do not try to live in it. God is writing his own beautiful story in your life and in your family member's lives. It doesn't matter how bad the situation seems, resurrection is the way of the Kingdom. Resurrection in your life first gives you faith and access.

"They triumphed over him by the blood of the Lamb and by the word of their testimony; they did not love their lives so much as to shrink from death." (Revelation 12:11)

This is our story. The more bleak the situation, the more powerful the testimony. Allow hope to be formed within you. We will experience a manifestation of heaven right here on earth in our most direct surroundings. When you see it happen in front of you, your expectation for more will increase. If you have seen it in your own home, won't you expect this in your church? Your training is practical, and it is for the benefit of others. You are blessed to be a blessing! Your training and breakthrough is for the breakthrough others are seeking.

Think about the families you really know, where you are allowed somewhat behind their closed doors. I'm sure you can confirm firsthand that families are struggling. As you commit to and allow for your own transformation and learn to walk in the Spirit with your family, what happened in Acts 2 will happen for you. You will be a light to your community and the Lord will add to your number every day. Your family will stand out! They will want your unity! They will ask for advice! They will ask for prayer! The world around you is attracted to unity because they were made for it as well!

Our churches and communities are extensions of our families, and neither will be changed until we are transformed. The Kingdom has come, now let us allow it to be formed within us until we see it manifest all around us. Our homes should start to resemble the Promised Land long before we can expect to cross into it.

CHAPTER 9:
A Joshua Army

On January 13th, 1982 Air Florida Flight 90 floundered upon takeoff from the Washington National Airport, crashed into a bridge and continued into the freezing Potomac River. Soon only the broken tail section remained afloat. Only six of the 79 passengers aboard survived the initial crash and were able to escape the aircraft as it sunk into the icy depths of the Potomac.

The six badly wounded passengers were in the struggle of their lives. After getting one man to safety, the helicopter threw a life-ring to 46 year old banker Arland Williams, who immediately gave it to the passenger next to him. Arland continued his selflessness and went on to assist in the rescue of the other five. By the time the helicopter made it back for him, he succumbed to his injuries. The 14th Street Bridge at the crash site would be renamed in his honor. Arland's heroism became a nationwide story at the time. In a moment no one planned, he used his last strength to serve others. Collectively five of the six remaining lives were saved because of the work of the rescue team and the sacrifice of one.

In 1 Corinthians 12 Paul describes how we each receive gifts for the benefit of others. We may feel like it takes everything in us to use these gifts, but unlike with Arland's final moments, they weren't designed to be a struggle to activate. Like in those fleeting moments on the Potomac, however, our activation can lead to many lives being saved.

"There are different kinds of gifts, but the same Spirit distributes them. There are different kinds of service, but the same Lord. There are different kinds of working, but in all of

them and in everyone it is the same God at work. Now to each one the manifestation of the Spirit is given for the common good. To one there is given through the Spirit a message of wisdom, to another a message of knowledge by means of the same Spirit, to another faith by the same Spirit, to another gifts of healing by that one Spirit, to another miraculous powers, to another prophecy, to another distinguishing between spirits, to another speaking in different kinds of tongues, and to still another the interpretation of tongues. All these are the work of one and the same Spirit, and he distributes them to each one, just as he determines." (1 Corinthians 12:1-11)

In his description of the gifts of the Holy Spirit, the Lord provides a recipe through Paul. The Lord is the giver of all gifts, what appears to be spiritual, and what appears to be natural. If we remain focused on the giver and recognize His sovereign working through our individual talents, we can make beautiful music. Not just music, but symphonies together that will attract the nations. As the spirit of this world continues to divide, through us the Lord is drawing together a unified army of the radically different and divinely gifted. This army will garner the attention it deserves, because it is of above. Our part is to work together using the gift He has given us.

WORKING TOGETHER

We see the gifts of the Spirit, collectively referred to as "signs and wonders," on display everywhere the Kingdom was preached as the early church advanced. The skepticism and bondage in people's lives is no less today, and perhaps much greater, so how much more the need for these to accompany our efforts today? But would we run a play in a game if we hadn't drilled it in practice? Rather, once we have mastered the play in practice, then we will run it in the game with confidence. Such is the case with the gifts. We must first learn together, functioning as a body ministering to one another and allowing the Spirit to build our confidence every step.

John Wimber, founder of the Vineyard movement, used to say "everybody gets to play." If we are His, we get to advance His Kingdom using the gifts. All of us. This is in contrast to a mindset that has hindered our progress. That mindset is to "leave it to the pros" and refer anyone with a need to the pastoral staff, causing everyone else to have an almost inactive role in ministry. This approach has hindered much of the work of the Kingdom and runs directly contrary to Jesus' own teachings.

In chapter 7 we learned the doctrine of the Nicolaitans was "power over the lay people." The root word here is Strong's 2992 laós, where we get the English term "laity." It is defined as a people, particularly used of "the people of the Lord." So when we later see Jesus rebuking the Laodicean chuch for being lukewarm or halfhearted, we see the same root word laós. The context is Revelation chapter 2 & 3 and we learn what started with power over the men and women of the church eventually becomes a lukewarm, inactive body. If we subscribe to the former, we become the latter.

Jesus summed up His stance on elevating men in the body.

"But do not be called Rabbi; for One is your Teacher, and you are all brothers. Do not call anyone on earth your father; for One is your Father, He who is in heaven. Do not be called leaders; for One is your Leader, that is, Christ. But the greatest among you shall be your servant. Whoever exalts himself shall be humbled; and whoever humbles himself shall be exalted." (Matthew 23:8-12)

How do our current structures fit with these words from Jesus?

These words, directly from our King, is a stinging indictment on our structures. The reality is we all need to see "regular folks" walking in the power of the Spirit, being salt and light.

As His co-heirs, we are ALL called off the bench and into "full time ministry." This does not mean we should quit our jobs and head off to seminary, rather see our true identity as His kings and priests on the earth and fulfill our calling.

As we take steps of faith and learn to function as a body together, we serve and lift each other up. In doing so, we practice the gifts in a safe environment of the true church of the body, connected to the Head with genuine interdependence on Him and each other. Greater steps of risk ensue. Continuing in 1 Corinthians 12, we see Paul's description of the gifts at work in a body.

"Just as a body, though one, has many parts, but all its many parts form one body, so it is with Christ. For we were all baptized by one Spirit so as to form one body—whether Jews or Gentiles, slave or free—and we were all given the one Spirit to drink. Even so the body is not made up of one part but of many.

"Now if the foot should say, 'Because I am not a hand, I do not belong to the body,' it would not for that reason stop being part of the body. And if the ear should say, 'Because I am not an eye, I do not belong to the body,' it would not for that reason stop being part of the body. If the whole body were an eye, where would the sense of hearing be? If the whole body were an ear, where would the sense of smell be? But in fact God has placed the parts in the body, every one of them, just as he wanted them to be. If they were all one part, where would the body be? As it is, there are many parts, but one body.

"The eye cannot say to the hand, 'I don't need you!' And the head cannot say to the feet, "I don't need you!" On the contrary, those parts of the body that seem to be weaker are indispensable, and the parts that we think are less honorable we treat with special honor. And the parts that are unpresentable are treated with special modesty, while our presentable parts need no special treatment. But God has put the body together, giving greater honor to the parts that lacked it, so that there should be no division in the body, but that its parts should have equal concern for each other. If one part suffers, every part suffers with it; if one part is honored, every part rejoices with it.

"Now you are the body of Christ, and each one of you is a part of it. And God has placed in the church first of all apostles, second prophets, third teachers, then miracles, then gifts of healing, of helping, of guidance, and of different kinds of tongues. Are all apostles? Are all prophets? Are all teachers? Do all work miracles? Do all have gifts of healing? Do all speak in tongues? Do all interpret? Now eagerly desire the greater gifts." (1 Corinthians 12:12-31)

We are one body. Could you imagine waking up to find that one of your body parts had decided not to participate for the day? Or how about if one decided to run the entire show? Either would lead to a very bad day. Now put this in context when we gather. Paul is painting a picture that will allow us to see a fuller picture of Christ. Mutual participation using the gifts of the Spirit.

"His intent was that now, through the church, the manifold wisdom of God should be made known to the rulers and authorities in the heavenly realms." (Ephesians 3:10)

The Greek word for manifold used here is *polypoikilos* (much varied, marked with a great variety of colors, of a painting). Our mutual participation is a brilliant display of many facets of God's wisdom. A painting with one color can be beautiful, but how much more so with a great variety of colors? Remember, this display is both for us and for the rulers in the heavenly realms!

When only one person speaks, we only see one reflection of God's wisdom. How then do we all participate to see His manifold wisdom on display? We honor each other, allowing each to share what God is showing them as we unite in the Spirit together. Let's not get tripped up by abuses from the past—this can and should be orderly because ours is a God of order.

Test what is shared to confirm they do not run contrary to anything in the written Word. Ask the Holy Spirit for the confirmation of a second witness. There is clearly much discovery as a part of this process, but one of our primary joys in this life (and the life to come) should be discovery.

"It is the glory of God to conceal a matter; to search out a matter is the glory of kings." (Proverbs 25:2)

Did you enjoy the game Hide-and-Seek as a child? How about following the clues on a scavenger hunt? We have learned the Lord sees us as His kings and priests unto Him, so this verse is now personal, directed at us. This verse is our destiny. It holds the key to unlock what it means to function in the gifts together. It is about discovering our identity together!

The world has long celebrated the "self-made man" and independence, but the Lord is teaching us the beauty and art of interdependence. As we depend on the Holy Spirit operating through one another, we learn to celebrate Him and each other. It literally helps us fulfill His summary of all the laws and commands (Love God, Love each other). Praise God—He has indeed given us a helper to guide us in this discovery process together!

DISCOVERING TOGETHER

A modern day example of the gifts in operation among a body of believers is found in the unnecessarily maligned Vineyard movement. Before Vineyard was even named, the story started with John Wimber's personal journey with the Holy Spirit.

After getting saved in a Bible study and eventually building a church, John took a somewhat traditional path to ministry. Where the story gets a little wild is when John allowed a young Evangelist to speak at the church in 1980. That evangelist was a man by the name of Lonnie Frisbee. Lonnie had also played a major role in the explosion of the Jesus movement less than a decade before, when God used him through signs and wonders to reach the "hippies." After Lonnie gave a nice talk that Sunday evening in Anaheim, he gave an altar call for all the youth to come forward in the church. Once up front, Lonnie invited the Holy Spirit to come. Pandemonium ensued.

The young people began to speak in tongues, some fell on the floor, and others simply shook. As this carried on beyond anyone's comfort level, some older congregation members slammed their Bibles closed and left the church. John was in a state of shock as the microphone fell from the stage and what appeared as babbling was broadcast through the gymnasium PA (they met in a high school gym at the time). The result was a divided congregation and a very puzzled Wimber. Even after heading up a division on church growth strategies at Fuller Theological Seminary for several years before this, Wimber did not have a context for what had just transpired.

John stayed up the entire night combing the scriptures for an answer. After not sleeping a wink, he received a phone call in the early morning from a pastor friend in Colorado. The pastor friend was also kept up all night with a word of knowledge from the Lord for John. The Word was three simple words: "It was me." That three-word confirmation changed everything for Wimber. Eventually it led to the young church going off on its own and launching the Vineyard movement, and Wimber and Frisbee would travel the country sharing what they were learning.

John's "discovery" approach to ministry became refreshment to a generation of believers entangled in a "legalistic" culture that pervaded the church of the 1980s. Even as you watch old videos of John's now famous "signs and wonders" classes at Fuller and Anaheim, you get the sense it was all about discovery for John. He had operated for so long from a place of maybe feeling like he knew a few things, that now he brought a refreshing humility to learning the ways of the Spirit.

John Wimber was very gifted at bringing others in on his process of learning what he called "God's ministry." John once recalled a story during his time of humbling, when the Lord said to him, "You've done your ministry. Now I'm going to teach you mine." One thing was clear. The Holy Spirit was the leader in these gatherings. John almost acted as a reporter. He would share experiences, inklings, and things they learned along their journey almost as clues that would lead to the next breakthrough.

Together, the young body of believers discovered ways the Holy Spirit liked to operate, but they always left room for the unusual. They cultivated an openness to new ways the Spirit wanted to teach them. I believe incorporating these methodologies would be beneficial to all of us.

HUMILITY

One of the roles of the Holy Spirit is teacher. As you have probably experienced, you can't teach someone who already knows it all. He wants us to function in humility and openness to learn His ways.

If you meet as a group and there is a primary facilitator, their recognition of the Holy Spirit as the leader and teacher sets the stage to do His ministry. I believe our leadership cultures, which run contrary to Jesus' own words: "call no man..." often box out the Spirit from leading us into breakthrough. He is the head; we are the body.

When we minister in the gifts as a group, we are inviting the very culture of heaven. We are asking for heaven to invade the earth where we are. The culture of heaven is His authority, His leadership, His presence. We need His power to do His ministry. His presence is His power, but will He manifest in our meeting as the leader if someone else is filling that role with all the answers?

"God opposes the proud but shows favor to the humble." (James 4:6)

I love John Wimber's story, because it is the story of a Christian leader who was humbled, and cultivated that posture of humility throughout the growth of the movement that ensued. Although John was a modern pioneer of the Spirit, he took many daggers from the Christian community. He was open about his own discovery process, but the majority rejected him.

God didn't reject John, however. The fruit of his ministry is even found in many of the great healing ministries of today. As you read the stories of Bill Johnson, Randy Clark, Heidi Baker and others, you find their common roots in John's groundbreaking work from the 1980s. I believe there was an endorsement from heaven on what John was doing and that was evidenced by the many reported healings, changed lives, and power encounters.

The gifts of the Spirit are for the building up of Christ's body. Any well-functioning body is a picture of interdependence. Each part relies on each other. This is what God's desire is for us. The definition of interdependence is *the dependence of two or more people or things on each other.* Matthew 18:20 speaks to this: **"For where two or three gather in my name, there am I with them."**

Every teaching on the gifts of the Spirit also speaks to this concept of interdependence. We were designed to depend on Him and on each other. This is displayed throughout creation, in the mystery of marriage, on display in machinery, and throughout our world.

Everything is connected, and so shall we be until we are the very picture of Oneness with Him. The church of the wilderness had much division, but the Promised Land is a place where we're united in Him. Let us seek this unity as we gather together in expectation. Let our unity and diversity be a sign to the divided world that our God is a God who unites and moves in power through His people.

CHAPTER 10:
Entering the Promised Land

Brian Chesky and Joe Gebbia were college friends turned struggling young San Francisco roommates. As income during the financial downturn became more scarce, it got so bad they sublet their own apartment to make rent. To maximize the rental income for the month, they did something different and unique. They purchased three air mattresses and rented to three guests needing a room for a visiting conference.

Within 12 months Airbnb was born. The humble startup struggled mightily for the first few years and nearly survived, but after identifying photos as a sticking point for interested renters they addressed the issue and their sky rocket journey began. The company is now valued at over $40 billion. They found an industry ripe for disruption and tapped into supply no one else realized existed. What is the moral of their underdog story? When opportunity meets need, explosive growth occurs. This is the backdrop for the coming global advance of the gospel.

Our current world appears in chaos. War, division and a disintegration of traditional values can cause the uninformed to speculate about darkness prevailing. Similar was the backdrop fifty years ago when the Jesus Movement sparked millions coming to Christ in the 1960's. A decade of sex, drugs and rock and roll somehow provided the perfect red carpet into the Kingdom. Despite the sense we have on the status of the world, God remains undeterred. His plans will be accomplished. This was the case with the obstinate children of Israel and it remains the case today.

THE KEYS TO THE KINGDOM

Returning our focus to the leader of our predecessors. After 120 years of experiencing countless miracles (40 of them spent leading a vast army of people through a barren wasteland) performed by God's hand and building a personal friendship with Him, Moses wanted more. More of God.

At that time I pleaded with the Lord..."You have begun to show to your servant your greatness and your strong hand...Let me go over and see the good land beyond the Jordan." (Deuteronomy 3:23-25)

God couldn't grant this request. His plan was already appointed to come through Joshua. Nonetheless, Moses communicated that after all these years he had only just started to see God's greatness! When we encounter God, all things feel new.

We are currently in a time when old age too often brings depression, cynicism and despair, but Moses' perspective brings us hope. When we have a friendship with God, we are constantly struck by His vastness. We can be in a constant state of simply wanting more of Him. This is hope. More of Him is why our journey and destination will never get boring.

How then, do we get to a place of experiencing more of God and yet even desiring more? In His final addresses to Joshua and the children of Israel, Moses hands over the keys to the Kingdom. These children of Israel could not use the keys, however. The Law was yet to be written on their hearts and they were yet to receive the Spirit, so they couldn't measure up.

The keys are for us today. A generation after the 40 Jubilees of our predecessors has been spent in the wilderness. The Law has been written on our hearts and the fire of the Spirit has been finishing its work of burning up all that separates us.

"Hear the decrees and laws...Follow them so that you may live and may go in and take possession of the land the LORD, the God of your ancestors, is giving you." (Deuteronomy 4:1)

Moses explained that following God's ways will lead to a successful life. The decrees and directives were for conquering and remaining. He continued:

"Observe them carefully, for this will show your wisdom and understanding to the nations...who will say 'Surely this great nation is a wise and understanding people.' What other nation...has their gods near them the way the Lord our God is near us whenever we pray to him?" (Deuteronomy 4:6-7)

As we observe His ways, our wisdom will be on display to the nations. They will be drawn to us and the God who grants us wisdom.

"But as for you, the Lord took you and brought you out of the iron-smelting furnace, out of Egypt, to be the people of his inheritance, as you now are." (Deuteronomy 4:20)

Moses made it clear the children of Israel were being prepared even before the journey. The time in Egypt serves as a type and shadow for us today. There is a time of preparation in the furnace before God can pour out the fullness of His plans. Our time has been the 40 Jubilees (almost 2,000 years) with the smelting furnace of the Holy Spirit, which has been working to prepare God's temple for full habitation.

"Keep his decrees and commands...so that you may live long in the land the Lord your God gives you <u>for all time</u>." (Deuteronomy 4:40)

Once again, at Verse 40 no less, we see God's plan to grant a permanent dwelling place to His people. The Promised Land has always been a type and shadow of God's true desire. Not to simply grant well maintained real estate to His people, but to establish a permanent dwelling place inside of us. This is an unconditional promise for His people and one that will last for all time. He does not change His mind—rather, His plans take time to come into their fullness.

In his closing moments as the appointed leader of the children of Israel, one of Moses' final acts was to summarize the Law and its associated blessings and curses. The children of Israel needed to hear it again before entering the Promised Land. He followed this by renewing their covenant with the Lord and prophesying about their future.

"When all these blessings and curses I have set before you come on you and you take them to heart wherever the Lord your God disperses you among the nations, and when you and your children return to the Lord your God and obey him with all your heart and with all your soul according to everything I command you today, then the Lord your God will restore your fortunes and have compassion on you <u>and gather you again from all the nations where he scattered you</u>…the Lord your God will circumcise your hearts and the hearts of your descendants, so that you may love him with all your heart and with all your soul, and live." (Deuteronomy 30:1-6)

The people were destined to disobey. Generations later, after God had scattered them among the nations, He would re-claim them all by His Spirit. He would circumcise our hearts so we could love Him with all of our hearts and souls, to then live. Our part is having the faith to believe this all to be true and to receive and respond with the love and life Moses foretold.

FAITH IS REQUIRED

Jesus Himself gave a cry of His heart in Luke 18:8 saying, "…when the Son of Man comes, will He find faith on the earth?" We find Jesus constantly rebuking His disciples for not having faith, and then He expresses this concern for all of us to see. We know from Hebrews 12 that a good Father disciplines those He loves, but what is the reason for the rebuke or discipline?

It is to spurn us on to more growth. Like a coach throwing down a challenge to a player, I sense the Lord saying, "Go for it! If you're not failing, you're not stretching yourself enough! Trust Me, have faith, take a risk, and do the things I did!" His heart's cry for us to have faith was clear, and the earth was always destined to be a place where a generation would rise up to fulfill the call.

MULTIPLICATION

Christian author Mike Arnold retells a story about an encounter with a donor in his book entitled *Uprising*. Mike's ministry has a preference of going deep into long periods of discipleship with a smaller number of people, but the donor was used to seeing large numbers of conversions from the ministries he supports. Struggling to make headway with the donor, Mike asked the Holy Spirit for help. At that moment, he felt the Spirit say, "run the numbers."

After the meeting, Mike did exactly that. He used generous estimates, assuming that if he started a new ministry to fulfill *part* of the great commission that it would grow by 1,000 new "decisions for Christ" each year (20 new people every Sunday), with a 25% retention rate. Now, say he could do this for just $100,000 a year *and* he could set up 100,000 identical ministries around the globe that could reproduce the same numbers. This would be amazing, right? These are numbers many ministries would dream about! Now let's say it were truly doable and reproducible. How long would it take to reach every man, woman and child on the earth? Even if the earth's population were to stop growing, it would take 280 years and $2,800,000,000,000. Add in population growth and there be nearly three times as many people born each year than we could ever reach. Ouch!

"All authority in heaven and on earth has been given to me. Therefore, go and make disciples of all nations, baptizing them in the name of the Father and of the Son and of the Holy Spirit, and teaching them to obey everything I have

commanded you. And surely I am with you always, to the very end of the age." (Matthew 28:18-20)

Now Mike contrasts that—a strategy being implemented almost across the board in the body of Christ currently—with one more similar to what Jesus demonstrated for us. The primary goal of this new ministry would be to live a life that reflects Christ. In reflecting Christ, if five people are drawn to the fruit of the Spirit in your life ,and ask how you have so much joy, you show them.

Now let us say you spend the next three years pouring into these five until Christ is truly formed in their lives. After these three years, the six of you go out and do the same, rolling this forward every three years with each person added. How long would it take in this scenario for the full great commission (making disciples) to be fulfilled? Amazingly, less than 39 years! That is counting population growth and even puts us 2 billion beyond our goal of every man, woman and child on earth. The cost: zero dollars!

GETTING OFF THE BENCH

Does the enemy want the body of Christ to recognize this opportunity? Certainly not! Instead, he wants us to live in a very small story, kind of like our dog Megan. Megan spends her days in a small space in our home with the occasional walk down our street. She does not know much different, so she is happy as long as she gets her little treats each day. She loves to spend time with us, her breakfast and dinner, the walks and getting her little doggie bites. In fact, her instincts for the doggie bites are so strong she forsakes the greatest desire of her heart (spending time with us). When it is time for her to go to bed at night, we have to coax her into her room so we can close the door. Without us calling out "treat," this would be impossible. Megan would fight, fuss, or run rather than go in that room! But when she gets close enough and we put out that treat, she willingly walks right in, following her nose and stomach every single time!

I always wonder what her feeling is when that door closes behind us. "Rats! Fell for it again." The other day I got a picture of this being the Christian life many of us live—really small lives that lack vision, because we are simply living for our little treats.

The enemy is all too happy to play into our small stories, offering us treats and closing the door behind us, with a plan to use the same tricks to do it all over again, day after day. Unlike dogs, we have the ability to open the door. If we lack the vision of how the Lord is calling us into our role in His great Story, as co-heirs in His Kingdom, I am afraid the enemy's tricks will continue to work on us.

"...in order that Satan might not outwit us. For we are not unaware of his schemes." (2 Corinthians 2:11)

If we are in genuine, vulnerable, discipleship relationships, surrendering our lives so that Christ can be formed in us, we will be aware of the devil's schemes. Why? Because we will be airing the lies in our heads to one another, gaining intel on the accuser and enemy of our souls.

In his famous 1942 work *The Screwtape Letters*, Christian author C.S. Lewis wrote a book from the enemy's perspective. In the book, Screwtape, an experienced tempter in Hell, guides a less experienced tempter (Wormwood) in his effort to draw his assigned patient away from the Enemy (God) and into the Underworld (Hell). Here are three quotes from the book that are profound and helpful as we plan to step out.

"Indeed the safest road to Hell is the gradual one—the gentle slope, soft underfoot, without sudden turnings, without milestones, without signposts...It is funny how mortals always picture us as putting things into their minds: in reality our best work is done by keeping things out."

These quotes are shared as a warning. The enemy has studied mankind for almost 6,000 years and developed strategies to thwart Christian initiative for the past 2,000 years. We need to be circumspect, aware, and sharing the dialogue in our heads with other "all-in" disciples so the lies can be dismantled. The enemy

147

strategy to distort Truth has always been the same.

"...for there is no truth in him. When he lies, he speaks his native language, for he is a liar and the father of lies." (John 8:44)

If we are in these relationships and we do fall, we will not fall victim to the lies again. *Where the Spirit of the Lord is there is freedom.* We did not receive a Spirit that deserts us when we fall short. The definition of sin is "missing the mark." Christ's sacrifice was sufficient to cover us for good. Sometimes we need that reminder—who better from than the ones we are called to have transparent and vulnerable relationships with.

"Two are better than one, because they have a good return for their labor: If either of them falls down, one can help the other up. But pity anyone who falls and has no one to help them up." (Ecclesiastes 4:9-10)

"For though the righteous fall seven times, they rise again..." (Proverbs 24:16)

This is a call to discipleship as our reasonable next step. To form groups, operate in the gifts, and to meet with one another until Christ is formed in us and the Kingdom is advanced all around us. Let's help our fellow Joshuas arise.

MAKING DISCIPLES

There are some brilliant strategies in the body right now on this very topic. In their book *Contagious Discipleship*, father and son disciple makers David and Paul Watson provide one of the best examples I have seen through forming what they call "Disciple-Making Movements." I highly recommend this book. If you do not have time to read, simply google "Discovery Bible Study." Your search results will provide you with many resources on how to host a Bible study for any small-size group that allows the Holy Spirit to lead. With the Spirit as the leader, these groups can multiply quickly and enable discipleship relationships to flourish!

Too many discipleship programs and techniques over-manage the environment, stopping the Holy Spirit from moving. Where the Spirit of the Lord is, there is freedom. If our discipleship method is a program that is not about freedom and discovery, guess what happens? No freedom, no Spirit. It becomes manufactured and growth is stifled rather than multiplied.

We don't have a product, we have Jesus. Even with empty rooms Chesky and Gebbia recognized their photos needed improvement for Airbnb to take off. Maybe we can recognize that love in an environment of freedom allows the Spirit to do the same?

"He has made us competent as ministers of a new covenant- not of the letter but of the Spirit; for the letter kills, but the Spirit gives life." (2 Corinthians 3:6)

The letter without the Spirit brings death. This is why so many Christians are struggling with a "double life." They are lacking the Spirit. I struggled with a double life for years until the Lord poured out His Spirit on me.

The Holy Spirit is a life-giving fire. Revival starts with that fire in you. If you are on fire, everyone you touch will catch fire. This is genuine discipleship. When a fire is kindling, people are drawn to and gather around that fire. Allow the Spirit to burn so brightly in you that as others are drawn in, they are set ablaze.

Is there anything holding me back from entering into discipleship relationships? How can these obstacles be eliminated?

Earlier we discussed how the primary work of the Holy Spirit is to "burn us up," with the end goal of making our whole temple Holy as He is Holy. No flesh enters in, so the blindfolds of flesh that we are wearing on this earth have to be dealt with.

When you think about it, every spiritual practice is illogical, from a human perspective. Tithing, serving, prayer, fasting, and worship all require faith, because they demonstrate a dependence on God to meet your needs rather than securing them yourself. Is our goal to get great at these spiritual practices, or is there even a higher calling as we live out the days of our pilgrimage on earth?

ONENESS

"My prayer is not for them alone. I pray also for those who will believe in me through their message, that all of them may be one, Father, just as you are in me and I am in you. May they also be in us so that the world may believe that you have sent me. I have given them the glory that you gave me, that they may be one as we are one— I in them and you in me—so that they may be brought to complete unity. Then the world will know that you sent me and have loved them even as you have loved me. Father, I want those you have given me to be with me where I am, and to see my glory, the glory you have given me because you loved me before the creation of the world. Righteous Father, though the world does not know you, I know you, and they know that you have sent me. I have made you known to them, and will continue to make you known in order that the love you have for me may be in them and that I myself may be in them." (John 17:20-26)

John 17:20-26 is the very end of Jesus' longest unbroken message in the gospels. It is literally the crescendo of a message and prayer that goes back almost five chapters. Upon finishing this last prayer, Jesus will be taken captive. Let us just say this is *the* major thing on His heart. What is His heart's cry? That we would be ONE! That we would be truly connected. It's the oneness the first church enjoyed when they ate and prayed together in unity and the Lord added to their number every day. It's also the oneness we will each enjoy with Him in our ultimate destiny of Tabernacles.

Like the unlikely Airbnb story, when opportunity meets need healthy things grow. The world we live in needs to see our love and unity in Christ. Being deeply connected to Him and each other is not only His greatest desire but the world's greatest need. It's literally what we were made for. His original intent expresses it (let us make man in our image), His design of family displays it (they will leave their father and mother and become one flesh), the greatest commandment demonstrates it (Love Him, Love each other), and our hearts cry out for it (to know and be fully known).

Of course, the adversary of all things God wants opposes it, perverting everything that brings unity into our lives (the holiness of His temple with sin, the sanctity of marriage with adultery and divorce, our love for Him and others with selfishness). But His Spirit in us is greater. It cries out "Abba, Father," and He is faithful to lead us in the connection and vulnerability with Him and others we were made for.

Let us enjoy this journey as the Lord gives us vision and pours out His love on us. Let us treat every day as a blank canvas for Him to paint a masterpiece on. His Kingdom is the kingdom of this world but "upside down." If you want to be great, be a servant. If you want joy, give it away first. If you need to be lifted up, lift Him up.

Whatever you want or need in this life must first be given away. It is His principle. It plays out throughout creation and even applies to the firstborn children (Exodus 13:2). It is contrary thinking, it is spiritual and not carnal. It requires an entirely new wineskin to even grasp. Living this way gets unlocked by living from within the well He has placed inside of us. Rather than gripping so tightly, we instead can live lighter and embrace the adventure with those He has put around us.

CLOSING WORDS OF ENCOURAGEMENT

Keep on taking risks! Be like a child as you step out in the supernatural Kingdom of life, and be willing to do the unusual. The most important thing in this life is not what others think of you or what you do, but who He is in you.

Stepping out where only He can come through will allow you to see into this beautiful mystery. Dream with God and embrace the pictures He gives you. These dreams and visions will keep you from living a small, insignificant life, and literally pull you right into your destiny. The dreams should always involve people, because His people are His purpose for us.

Be patient and forgiving of yourself during this process, though! Building genuine character takes time. How much time did it take for you to become conformed to the pattern of this world? Years of television-watching, internet-surfing, time spent with people who love the things of this world, etc. This time often far outweighs the time we need to have our minds renewed. Transformation is a process, so be patient with it. It requires surrender, so give each day to Him and invest your time rather than spending it.

"Then the angel showed me the river of the water of life, as clear as crystal, flowing from the throne of God and of the Lamb down the middle of the great street of the city. On each side of the river stood the tree of life, bearing twelve crops of fruit, yielding its fruit every month. And the leaves of the tree are for the healing of the nations. No longer will there be any curse. The throne of God and of the Lamb will be in the city, and his servants will serve him. They will see his face, and his name will be on their foreheads. There will be no more night. They will not need the light of a lamp or the light of the sun, for the Lord God will give them light. And they will reign for ever and ever." (Revelation 22:1-5)

Eden is restored, my friends. Even now, in Christ, we are once again as if we never ate the fruit. The tree of life was guarded in the garden after the fall, but in John 15 Jesus said, "I am the true vine." Jesus has undone the curse. As we abide in Him, His nature becomes ours and the result is fruit.

Intimacy and relationship with the Lord becomes our way of life. It releases authority to bring His healing to the nations. I pray that you will be awakened to the authority you possess as you abide in Him. I pray you will move past all barriers and obstacles in your own life and begin to shift cities, regions, and nations with your God-given authority. His living water is meant to not just flow into you, but through you.

The enemy has too long lulled the world of Christianity into inactivity and slumber through religious doctrines that promote fear and a "bunker" mentality. Too many sermons and too much of our theology are based on a fictitious "Left Behind" book and movie series depicting the world as going to hell in a handbasket. What has been the fruit of this message? Hunker down, stock up, get ready for the enemy to reign until the Lord returns! Did Christ demonstrate what it looks like to conquer, and charge us to do the same to the ends of the earth, only for us to hide and play it safe?

What end time Christian worldview have I believed? What has been the fruit of this in my life?

Rather than getting stuck in doctrine that does not produce fruit, let's look at what is actually taking place. There is clear momentum toward a significant move of the Holy Spirit in our generation. This move is the move out of the wilderness and the crossing over into the Promised Land.

If we see the kingdom of darkness on display, how much more should we anticipate the Kingdom of Light breaking through those clouds with power! Let us take a step back again and take the long view of what has transpired since our Lord's resurrection:

33 AD	3,000 added at Pentecost
33-100AD	Early church enjoys unity and Kingdom advances
33 - today	Outsiders creep in and dilute the message
200-1500	Few revivals or masses moved by the Spirit
1450	Printing press invented
1517	Start of Protestant Reformation
1525	First English language Bible translation
1730	First wave of revivals hits with Protestants in U.S.
1730	- today Five more waves of revival led by Holy Spirit

It is fascinating to look at Christian history from this high up, as we ponder why the ways of the Kingdom haven't truly yet advanced through our nations, communities or even churches.

Did the lack of truth or availability of the Bible play a role? It is amazing the printing press, translation of the Bible and reformation all happened in the same era. We can see now how that era has helped with God's plan to bring us out of the wilderness. Since that time, revivals have been breaking out as heaven has been breaking through. We live in the tension between the two kingdoms as ambassadors of His. Looking at the history reminds me of Jesus' words on the clashing of kingdoms.

"The kingdom of heaven has been subjected to violence, and violent people have been raiding it." (Matthew 11:12)

It is now our time of advancing, not trying to force our views on others or demanding our laws get passed, but rather, using the blueprint Jesus provided for us. The advance has begun and it has been in waves of truth that God is releasing on the earth.

There have now been six revival periods or waves of revival during this period, each with demonstrations of the Kingdom with signs and wonders. There seems to be a spiritual momentum or "build-up" to a massive seventh wave in our generation, which is both our Sabbath and crossing over into the Promised Land. This wave will lead to significant reformation and usher in the greatest harvest of all time as the church unites.

The word "reformation" is used often in Christian circles. It is used in a historical sense, regarding what happened in the early 1500s, and in a prophetic sense about what God is going to do again.

If the first reformation was a type and shadow of things to come, which is God's oft-used pattern, then let us look at the first as an example. God didn't actually reform anything, He raised up a new standard. The new standard in the 1500s was based on the truth of His Word. It was incomplete, however, and led to factions that caused thousands of divisions.

Like the Marines who stepped foot onto the shores of Hawaii before its annexation, now is the time for the good ambassadors to claim the King's domain. The new standard we will see in the coming reformation will be marked by fullness rather than factions. Fullness of the gifts, fullness of joy and fullness of unity will abound because of the fullness of His Spirit in this move.

Let us fast and pray together as the day approaches. The greatest need of our world today is a mighty manifestation of the Spirit of God in transformative power. It is coming. Those of us who surrender to the King's good ways will be both recipients and participants in this great and endless wave that ushers in God's glory.

Lord, let the wave of your Spirit come and carry us out of the wilderness and into our destiny! Let your Joshuas arise! Your Kingdom come, your will be done, on earth as it is in heaven!

ABOUT THE AUTHOR

Joseph Worth is a modern reformer, speaker and Kingdom entrepreneur who dreams with God and desires to bring Heaven's strategies to earth and help others to do the same.

References

NY Post 11/22/15 "Man's incredible survival journey."

Wikipedia – Jim Elliot

Wikipedia – William Wallace

Wikipedia – Prince Kaboo

Wikipedia – Eric Lidell

Wikipedia – The Cost of Discipleship

http://listverse.com/2013/01/15/the-top-10-most-inspiring-self-sacrifices/

Uprising, Mike Arnold, Nikao Press; 2 edition (May 19, 2016)

Contagious Disciple Making, David and Paul Watson, Thomas Nelson (December 23, 2014)

Made in the USA
Middletown, DE
20 December 2021

55722479R00096